SIMPLY
KOSHER

RAMONA BACHMANN

gefen גפן
publishing house בית הוצאה לאור

Gefen Publishing House Ltd.   Gefen Books
POB 36004, Jerusalem   12 New St., Hewlett
91360 Israel   N.Y., U.S.A. 11557
972-2-5380247   516-295-2805

Translated from the Danish *Mit Joediske Koekken*

Illustrations: Susanna Hartmann

Photos: Soeren Bay Clausen

Cover Design: Helen Twena/Gefen

Cover Photo: Roni Matityahu (Paëlla dish, p. 62)

Typesetting: Marzel A.S. - Jerusalem

ISBN 965 229 104 8

Edition 9 8 7 6 5 4 3 2

Printed in Israel

Send for our free catalogue

About the Author

Ramona Bachmann

Ramona Bachmann, a complete autodidact in gastronomy, is celebrated in Denmark for having written a superbly received cookbook. Born in Bombay, Ramona grew up in the Jewish quarter, where her mother had already achieved renown for her extraordinary cooking.

At fifteen, Ramona left India for Israel, where she graduated from an agricultural high school and was educated in Israel's fast developing hotel and tourist industry.

Ramona Bachmann has lived in Denmark for 28 years, where she has taught Hebrew, Jewish heritage and kosher cooking at the Jewish day school in Copenhagen. She has written a food column for the leading Jewish monthly magazine.

In addition to preparing gourmet dinners in her own home, Ramona has been in charge of numerous spectacular Jewish catered affairs, where guests' compliments have motivated her to commit her cooking expertise to paper.

This cookbook reflects a true harmony of East and West, old and new, refinement and simplicity. Throughout the book one finds an atmosphere of quality and personal devotion to good taste, important for entertainment as well as daily purposes.

The readers will discover what has already been witnessed by Danish reviewers: Jewish gastronomy – within kosher guidelines – is surprisingly varied and delicious.

Calendar

Gregorian Calendar	Jewish Calendar		
Month	*Month*	*Day*	*Holiday*
Sept./Oct.	Tishrei	1-2	Rosh Hashanah (Jewish New Year)
		10	Yom Kippur (Day of Atonement)
		15-21	Sukkoth (Feast of Booths)
		21	Hoshanah Raba
		22	Shemini Atzeret
		23	Simchat Tora
Oct./Nov.	Cheshvan		
Nov./Dec.	Kislev	25--2	Hannukah (Festival of Lights)
Dec./Jan.	Tevet		Hannukah
Jan./Feb.	Shvat	15	Tu B'Shvat (New Year for Trees)
Feb./March	Adar	14	Purim (Feast of Lots)
March/April	Nissan	15-22	Pesach (Passover)
April/May	Iyar	5	Yom Ha'atzmaut (Israel Independence Day)
		18	Lag Ba'Omer
		28	Yom Yerushalayim (Jerusalem Day)
May/June	Sivan	6-7	Shavuot (Feast of Weeks)
June/July	Tammuz		
August	Av	9	Tishah B'Av
Aug./Sept.	Elul		

Contents

7

The Real Meaning of
Jewish Cuisine...

It is a common assumption that the most popular topic of conversation is the weather. Everyone talks about it, but nobody does anything about it, we say.

The truth is probably that everyone talks about the weather, but since nothing can be done about it, the topic is quickly exhausted. And this is why the weather as a topic of conversation is clearly surpassed by food, since that is one thing we can always do something about.

The two subjects are not completely unrelated: Climatic conditions have helped form our eating habits, and specialties differ from country to country. Jewish cooking has its origin in Israel, the cradle of Judaism. It has developed many variations as Jews settled in different parts of the world. The specialties of European Jews are completely different to those of the Oriental Jews. And even the little Danish Jewish community has developed its own cuisine.

And so it is truly significant that Ramona Bachmann, who has literally inhaled the smoke in kitchens of many countries, has written what can justifiably be called an international Jewish cookbook.

What is decisive is that it is a *Jewish* cookbook. Jews have always put great emphasis on what they eat. This is partly because of Biblical rules, which are described briefly in this book, and partly because Jewish celebrations have always been accompanied by good food. Even though the Bible emphasizes that man does not live by bread alone, Jews have never been ascetics. Poverty might have made it necessary to eat frugally during the week, but when the Sabbath or holidays came, people gathered for a festive meal.

The sense of community at the dining table did not come simply from the enjoyment of eating. The meal developed into a service of worship, and Jewish traditions made the table the successor to the altar that had stood in the Temple. The woman who prepared the meal was not considered a menial laborer; she was a servant of the Temple. And so the results of her endeavors were naturally not a matter of indifference.

Ramona Bachmann's book will help the Temple servants of both sexes to make the sense of community around the dining table a source of even greater joy and glory to God.

Bent Melchior

Chief Rabbi of Denmark

"...Greenery is coming up and the herbs of the mountains are being harvested. . . and there is enough goat's milk for your food and the food of your household. . ."
Proverbs, Chapter 27, Verses 25, 27

Simply Kosher – An Idea Simmering!

The book you see here is the culmination of a long journey. It took form as I traveled from country to country throughout the world. In each place, I looked for the special taste of Jewish homes. I sampled what I found, and adapted what I could as I moved on.

My childhood began in Bombay, where my mother would prepare wonderful dishes under the most primitive conditions. The rich colors, flavors and aromas which surrounded me in India are still with me today. As a young girl, I moved to Israel on my own. My first home was an agricultural school where I lived, worked and studied. My introduction to prepared, institutional food came when I was assigned to serve meals in the school's dining hall. Later I chose a career in the tourist industry. That's when I got the chance to travel and sample the cuisine at the cafés and restaurants in many countries. Then I married, and settled in "Wonderful, Wonderful Copenhagen". This marked a new stage in my journey.

Up until my marriage, my relationship to food and cooking had been pretty one-sided: I knew what I liked, and I had learned how to order it from any menu in almost any language! Only as I began married life did I realize that

there was another side to this story – one might also be expected to cook!

Since cooking hadn't been one of the skills listed on my resume, the first cook in our home was my husband. I was quite impressed by the variety of the meals he served: soup, cold cuts, french fries, fruit and cheese platters and more. Every dish was attractively garnished and served in a spotless kitchen. Eventually I learned the reason that the kitchen stayed so clean: the pots and pans were never touched! In addition to the soups, which had come from powdered mixes, all of the food we ate in those early days had been prepared and packaged long before it reached our table.

Soon I developed a longing for "real" food. I was pretty embarrassed that I'd never learned one of the most valuable skills in life – how to cook! It was, however, some consolation that I knew precisely how good food was supposed to taste.

I began the arduous process of working my way through Danish cookbooks, constantly asking friends and family for advice. The results of my first efforts were not always what I'd had in mind, but with my husband's encouragement, I kept on experimenting. My friends and relatives soon became the hapless

9

victims of my experiments. Their reactions must not have been too discouraging, since I soon took up cooking as a hobby and, later, made it my profession.

For several years, I taught kosher cooking at the Caroline Jewish School in Copenhagen. In this role, I had the opportunity to help my students prepare themselves for the day when they would be faced with a shelf full of spotless pots and pans in the brand new kitchens of their future homes.

Through my monthly food column for a Jewish newspaper in Denmark, I enriched my understanding of kosher cooking and the endless variety of individual taste.

This book not only contains recipes, but places them in a context with descriptions of many rich Jewish traditions that we hope will enhance your cooking and eating experience.

This book could not have been written without the help of a number of very devoted people.

I'd like to thank Chief Rabbi Bent Melchior and Rabbi Bent Lexner, of Denmark, for their help in reviewing and editing the pages which deal with Jewish law and tradition.

Thanks also to my mother, who "spoiled" me with excellent cooking, and later taught me what I needed to know about spices and other vital ingredients of **Simply Kosher**.

Special credit goes to my friends, Nilly, Maxine and Rhea for editorial guidance.

Finally, thank you to relatives and friends who have sampled, criticized and collaborated in order to keep this book going on the back burner until ready to be served.

It is my warmest wish that this book will become an inspiration to those who wish to live according to our Jewish dietary laws, which turn out to be in perfect harmony with the modern science of nutrition.

Enjoy!
Ramona Bachmann

Kashrut
Jewish Dietary Laws

The word **kashrut**, or **kosher**, is used to describe traditional Jewish Dietary laws.

Kosher means suitable. That is, food which is acceptable according to the ancient and traditional rules of Judaism.

There are 613 guidelines *(mitzvot)* by which Jews are expected to abide. At least fifty of them relate to food and eating.

The most significant dietary laws are as follows:

1. All things that are grown from the earth – fruit, vegetables, spices, etc. – are permissible foods. The same applies to milk and milk products from permissible mammals and eggs from permissible birds.

2. Mammals which can be eaten are those which both chew their cud and have cloven hooves – that is, no pork, horse or camel.

3. The only birds which can be eaten, according to tradition, are chickens, geese, ducks, doves and turkeys – no birds of prey.

4. The only fish which can be eaten are those which have scales and fins.

5. No shellfish or mollusks may be eaten.

MEAT AND DAIRY

One of the surest signs of a kosher kitchen is the separation of meat and dairy.

This rule means that there are two separate sets of dishes, utensils, pots, pans, etc., in every kosher kitchen.

There are three different instances in the Bible where we read:

"You must not cook a calf in its mother's milk" (Exodus 23:19, Exodus 34:26 and Deuteronomy 14:21).

According to this law we are forbidden:

a. To cook milk or milk products together with meat or meat products;

b. To eat milk and meat together, including any combination of milk products and meat products;

c. To profit or derive income from such a combination.

For this reason we must distinguish carefully between three different food groups: MEAT, DAIRY and PARVE (neutral) products.

1. MEAT PRODUCTS

These are defined as any food products prepared from beef or poultry, including any soups, sauces, etc. made from animals. All meat products must be from permissible animals, and the rules for slaughtering must be followed (see page 14).

Gelatin from animal bones must not be used. However, there are several alternatives which are acceptable under kosher law.

Agar-agar – extracted from algae. This can be purchased in a health food store.

Ardi Powder – extracted from fish bones. This is an Israeli product and is available in many kosher food stores throughout the world.

Pectine or malamine - extracted from fruits and plants. This product is best suited for fruit desserts.

In addition, a new kosher gelatin substitute is now being developed that is an extract of fish skin.

After eating meat and before eating any dairy products, one must wait a minimum of one to six hours, according to local rabbinic guidelines.

2. DAIRY PRODUCTS

Foods which contain milk, butter, or other dairy derivatives are considered to be dairy products and therefore can be served only with dairy meals.

Milk should be from permissible animals in order to be considered kosher. Dairy foods must not contain any animal or meat products.

Many desserts contain milk or dairy products, and are therefore considered dairy food.

Gelatin substitutes or thickening agents which include any meat products or derivatives, must not be used when preparing dairy products.

If one has drunk a dairy product (such as coffee with milk), it is acceptable to eat meat products after rinsing the mouth.

If you have eaten a hard cheese, you may not eat meat for at least one hour afterwards.

3. PARVE PRODUCTS

Food products not belonging to the meat or dairy groups are considered *parve* (neutral). Parve foods include: eggs, fish, fruit, vegetables and grains.

Parve foods can be prepared, served and eaten together with meat or dairy foods, but only with the appropriate dishes and utensils.

SPECIAL RULES

Eggs should be of permitted birds, such as hens, ducks, geese, turkey, etc. No eggs of birds of prey are acceptable under kosher law.

Eggs should be checked for blood. To do this, one breaks the egg into a separate glass, rather than directly into the mixing bowl used for the entire recipe. If even a tiny speck of blood is found, the egg must be disposed of and the glass must be washed thoroughly.

Fish: All fish roe must come from kosher fish (those with fins and scales).

Fruit, vegetables and grains must be thoroughly checked for worms and insects before being used in cooking.

Oil and Margarine should be made from 100% vegetable oil. Some shortenings may include milk powder or butter and are therefore considered dairy foods and are not parve.

Many of the meat recipes call for margarine. Make sure to check that the margarine you use is parve, and does not carry a small "D" for dairy.

"But flesh with its life, which is its blood, you shall not eat."
Genesis, Chapter 9, Verse 4

"Only be sure that you do not eat the blood, for the blood is life and you may not eat the life with the meat. You shall not eat it, you shall pour it upon the earth like water."
Deuteronomy, Chapter 12, Verses 23, 24

Shechita: Kosher Slaughtering

There are many laws which pertain to kosher slaughtering and cleaning meat, both beef and poultry. Slaughtering is to be performed by specially trained butchers, **shochtim**, working under the close supervision of the local rabbinate. The knife used must be extremely sharp, with a smooth, unnicked blade, in order to prevent cruelty to the animal being slaughtered.

According to the laws of kosher slaughter, a prayer is said while the arteries of the animal's neck are cut in one swift movement. The air and food passages are cut simultaneously, ensuring a rapid and painless death, as well as the thorough bleeding required for cleansing purposes.

Once slaughtered, the animal is cut up and examined thoroughly. If the butcher detects any illness in or around the animal's innards, the animal is declared unsuitable for consumption.

This procedure is followed for both beef and poultry.

The Bible places much emphasis on the prohibition against consuming any blood, as well as the fat known as *"chelev"*. At the butcher's, the blood, the veins and the membrane with the forbidden fat are removed. Because it is much more difficult to remove these parts from the hind quarters of an animal, many Jewish communities do not allow consumption of meat from the hind quarters. In order to remove any residual blood, the meat is soaked in lukewarm water for at least one half hour, and then soaked in salt water for one more hour. The meat is then rinsed 2 to 3 times in cold water.

Kosher meat is available at butcher shops and special meat counters in some supermarkets or delicatessens. Note that liver must be slashed, broiled and then rinsed of any excess blood, before being used in kosher cooking.

The Jewish Year

The Hebrew calendar is a complicated one, based both on the cycles of the moon as well as the sun. In contrast, the Gregorian calendar, common throughout most of the Western world, is a solar one – based only on the sun. The Mohammedan calendar, used in the Islamic world, is purely lunar.

According to the Hebrew calendar, a new month begins with each new moon. Yet the seasons of the sun must also be calculated, in order to ensure that holidays and festivals fall at the appropriate time of year. Thus, the luni-solar calendar, used by the Jewish people since ancient times, has the task of balancing between the 365 days of the solar year and the 354 lunar days. In order to adjust for this, the Hebrew calendar adds an entire month during leap years. Purely lunar months have 29½ days. The Hebrew months have either 29 or 30 days and, according to the complex calculations of this calendar, the same month may vary from 29 to 30 days in different years.

Each **24-hour day** is calculated from sunset to sunset. Thus each holiday begins at sundown and ends at sundown – the next evening.

The **Hebrew week** begins on Saturday evening (at the end of the Sabbath) with a beautiful ceremony called "Havdala". Sunday is called "Day One" in Hebrew, Monday is "Day Two" and so on, each of the week days counting down to the Sabbath.

There are two ways to count the months of the year: One may begin with the month of *Nissan*, in the Spring, based on our ancestors' liberation from bondage in Egypt. Or, one may start at the Hebrew New Year, which falls during the month of Tishrei in the Fall (following the last harvest of the year). Tishrei is traditionally believed to be the time of the creation of the world.

The **Hebrew months** are:

Tishrei, Cheshvan (Fall)

Kislev, Tevet, Shvat, Adar (Winter)

During leap years, the additional month of *Adar Sheni* is added.

Nissan, Iyar, Sivan (Spring)

Tammuz, Av, Elul (Summer)

The years of the Hebrew calendar are counted from Year 1, beginning with the creation of Adam. The year from September 1993 to September 1994 corresponds to the Hebrew year, 5754.

Family Celebrations

"**Simcha**", happiness, is a theme which is repeated often in Judaism. Family celebrations, called simchas, are of great significance throughout each Jewish life. When an individual celebrates, his whole family and community participate in the joy of celebration. Events celebrated in the synagogue include births, the confirmation (bar and bat mitzvah), the wedding ceremony and other special events.

Every healthy baby boy born into a Jewish family is to be circumcised when he is eight days old. This custom originated with Abraham, the Biblical patriarch, who was commanded to circumcise himself and his offspring, in order to make a pact with God. *Brit* means pact. The **Brit Milah**, or circumcision, is carried out by a trained practitioner, licensed by the religious community, called a **Mohel**. The brit signifies a commitment and entry into the Jewish community. The family hosts a festive meal which often includes greens and fish, traditional symbols of life and happiness. For newborn girls there is no circumcision, but often a naming ceremony is held in the synagogue, followed by a toast or festive meal hosted by the family.

A special ceremony, called **Pidion Haben**, is held 30 days after the birth of a first-born son. "Pidion Haben" means "the ransom of the son". This custom dates back to the time of the ancient Jewish Temple, when the first-born son was to be dedicated to a holy life serving in the Temple. Since then, there has been a tradition of ransoming, or buying back, the son's freedom to pursue a more secular life. At this ceremony, a silver coin is symbolically given to a descendant of the high priest, who then releases the child from his debt of holy service, returning him to the care of his family.

The Jewish child's entry to adulthood is marked at age 13 for boys, and 12 for girls. In the **Bar Mitzvah** ceremony held in the synagogue, boys recite blessings and then read a section of the Torah, or Bible, an honor reserved for adults. From now on, the boy will be counted as a full member of the community and will be expected to join in prayers, wearing a *talit* (a prayer shawl) and *tefilin* (the traditional phylacteries). The Bat Mitzvah celebration for girls is similar to the Bar Mitzvah. In both cases, blessings and toasts are given at a reception in the synagogue, and a family celebration can be held as well. In some communities, the coming of age is celebrated for both boys and girls at age 14 or 15 with a confirmation ceremony and special prayer service.

The **wedding ceremony** is considered to be the most joyous event in a Jewish life. The wedding vows are recited under a special canopy, called a *chuppa*, often in a synagogue. A rabbi marries the happy couple, surrounded by family and friends. The groom places a ring on the bride's finger and the wedding contract (the "*ketubah*") is read aloud. A blessing is said as the couple sips from a ceremonial cup of wine. Then the groom crushes a glass, to symbolize the fact that even at the most joyful occasion, we remember the destruction of the ancient Temple. Speeches and songs of prayer follow, accompanied by a festive meal and dancing and singing. Seven days of festive meals ("*sheva brachot*") follow.

"Remember the Sabbath day, to keep it holy. Six days shall you labor, and do all your work; but the seventh is a Sabbath to the Lord your God . . ."
Exodus, Chapter 20, Verses 8-10

Shabbat

The Hebrew word for the Sabbath, *Shabbat*, comes from the word *shevet* – to sit, or rest. It marks the seventh day of Creation, the day on which God sat and rested from his labors – stopping to look at what had been created during the first six days of the world. According to the Hebrew calendar, Shabbat falls on Saturday, Sunday being the first day of the new week.

Shabbat is the only holiday mentioned by name in the Ten Commandments. The fourth commandment instructs us clearly about what to do on the Sabbath: to rest and avoid all forms of work. Instead, the day should be used to enrich our minds – both intellectually and spiritually.

Shabbat begins before sundown on Friday and lasts 25 hours until Saturday evening. This means that the time that the Sabbath begins and ends differs from one week to the next throughout the year.

Because we are forbidden to work on Shabbat, foods to be eaten on Shabbat must be prepared in advance. When the days are long, there is plenty of time on Friday to prepare the Shabbat meals.

However, in the winter months, some of the tasty Shabbat specialties are best prepared on Thursday and reheated right before Shabbat.

Electrical appliances are not to be turned on on Shabbat. Therefore, food which is to be eaten hot should be kept warm in the oven, or on an electric hot plate (lit before Shabbat begins).

Shabbat is a festive day when the family traditionally gathers together for good meals. **Three meals** are eaten in the course of Shabbat: Friday evening dinner, Saturday lunch (which follows morning prayers) and a third meal (called *seuda shlishit*) which is eaten before sundown on Saturday evening.

On **Friday evening** a festive table is set, with a tablecloth, flowers and two candles. The candles are lit by the woman of the house just before sundown. She recites a blessing and says a special prayer for her family members. The menu includes wine, two loaves of the special Shabbat bread, challah, fish and/or meat and more. Even families with the most limited incomes try to serve the best at this meal, in order to create a special Shabbat atmosphere.

According to tradition, **the first meal on Saturday** is served only after the morning prayers have been completed. Therefore, many have a piece of cake with a cup of coffee or tea before going to synagogue for morning services on Saturday. This tradition makes for an extra keen appetite, and therefore it's wise to have lunch ready as soon as everyone returns from synagogue.

In the summer, there is often a cold meal ready for lunch, while in winter, a casserole called Hamin is served.

Hamin is a one-pot meal which has been kept warm in the oven overnight (see page 28).

The lovely aroma of this slow-cooked meal fills the kitchen and greets the family as they return from synagogue.

Following the filling lunch, some good reading and a nap often round out a peaceful Shabbat afternoon.

The **third meal** is usually a light dairy meal. At the end of Shabbat, there is a special parting ceremony, called *Havdala* – or the separation – which divides the holy Shabbat from the work week. The Havdala ceremony includes a · twisted candle, a cup of wine and an ornamental spice box.

The fragrant spices in the spice box are especially aromatic, and they are used to symbolize the idea that the peaceful Shabbat atmosphere should linger throughout the week. As this ceremony comes to an end, everyone wishes one another a week of health and happiness.

Challah

Braided Bread

Makes 4 loaves

PARVE

Ingredients:

50 g (2 oz) yeast
2 cups lukewarm water
2 eggs
1 tbs salt
2 tbs oil
2 tbs sugar
Approx. 1 kg (2 lbs) white
  flour
½ egg for crust

Garnish:

Poppyseeds

Challah is mentioned in the Bible, in the book of Numbers: "You shall make a gift to the Lord from the first yield of your baking throughout generations." (Numbers, 15:18-21) When forming the dough for bread, one piece of the dough is taken out and a blessing is said over it. This portion is then baked and allowed to burn in the oven, ensuring that it will not be eaten, as it is to serve as an offering. The name for this offering of dough, challah, actually means: the portion taken out.
Challah is the traditional Shabbat bread – softer and sweeter than the bread eaten during the week.

Directions:

Crumble the yeast in lukewarm water with one teaspoon of sugar. Let stand 5 minutes.

Add the rest of the sugar, salt, egg and oil and stir well. The flour is added a little at a time, and the dough is kneaded until it slips easily from your hands.

Set in a bowl and cover with a damp cloth. Let rise for 40-45 minutes. Knead dough on a floured table.

Divide into 4 balls. Divide each ball into 3: Roll each into a long rope and braid these three ropes together. Cover the challah with a damp cloth and leave it to rise again on a paper-covered baking tin for about 15-20 minutes.

Brush with egg and sprinkle with poppyseeds, if desired. Bake at 200°C (400°F) for about 30 minutes, until golden brown on top.

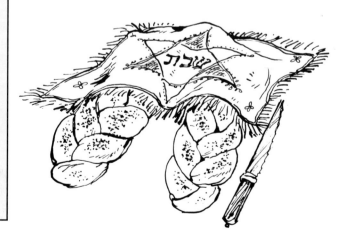

MEAT

"Great Gehackte!"
Chopped Liver with Avocado
Serves 8

Ingredients:
500 g (1¼ lb) calf's liver
4 tbs parve margarine
2 tbs chicken fat
4 onions, sliced thick
4 hard-boiled eggs
3 ripe avocados
½ cup prepared bouillon
Salt and pepper to taste

Garnish:
Hard-boiled egg
Parsley and avocado

Directions:
Melt the margarine and chicken fat in a pan. Slice liver and onion and fry.

Grind the fried liver, onions, hard-boiled eggs and peeled avocado in a meat grinder. Mix in the bouillon and fat from the pan; salt and pepper to taste.

Arrange in portions and decorate with boiled egg, chopped parsley and thin avocado slices. Serve chilled.

MEAT

Chopped Liver with Egg
Serves 6

Ingredients:
500 g (1¼ lb) calf's liver
1 large onion
4 tbs parve margarine
3 tbs chicken fat
3 eggs
Salt and pepper to taste

Directions:
Cut the liver and onion into small pieces and fry well in margarine.

Cook eggs for 10 minutes. Peel.

Grind the liver, eggs and onion – feeding these ingredients once through a meat grinder.

Add melted chicken fat, the fat from the frying pan, salt and pepper. Mix well together and arrange on a small plate or in portions. Serve chilled.

Here are two different recipes for a Shabbat favorite, Chopped Liver.
Note: In kosher cooking, liver must be seared on an open flame in order to ensure that all blood is removed before cooking. The name for the first dish was inspired by my sister-in-law's enthusiasm for gehackte leber (chopped liver). She yelled, "Great Gehackte!" when she first tasted my version of the familiar dish, prepared with liver and avocado.

Salmon Pâté

Serves 8

PARVE

Ingredients:
1 kg (2 lbs) salmon
500 g (1¼ lb) fish fillets (cod, flounder, or any other kosher, lean fish)
6 egg yolks
6 egg whites
Salt
2 tsp white pepper
½ cup dry white wine or fish broth
2 tbs flour
1 tbs lemon juice
½ cup chopped dill, chives or parsley
¼ cup chopped capers
2 carrots (boiled 10 minutes)
Parve margarine for the mold

Garnish:
Lime, watercress, tomatoes

Sauce:
½ cup mayonnaise
2 tbs lemon juice
2 tbs chopped herbs
½ cup capers
½ cup fish broth
Salt and pepper

Directions:
Bone and skin the salmon (most fish markets are glad to help with this chore). Save the bones for broth.

Chop the salmon and fish fillet well, by feeding them through a meat grinder twice. Add all ingredients except the egg whites, carrots and margarine.

Beat the egg whites until they are semi-stiff and fold into the fish batter.

Grease a loaf pan or other mold with margarine and pour in half the fish.

Arrange the whole carrots in the middle and pour the rest of the fish on top.

Cover the mold with tin foil and place the mold inside a large pan of water in the oven.

Bake at 180°C (350°F) for 45 minutes.

Cool the pâté, preferably for 12 hours or more.

Meanwhile, combine all the sauce ingredients. Mix well until the sauce is smooth.

Turn the pâté out onto a platter, or serve in individual portions with garnish and sauce.

Be sure to surround the mold with water while baking. Chill the paté after baking.
To remove Pâté from the Mold:
Dip the pan or mold into hot water briefly to loosen the contents.
In one swift motion, turn the pan over onto a platter for serving.

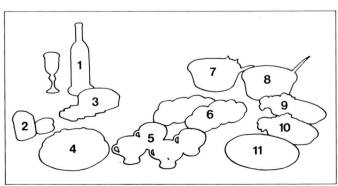

Shabbat

Chatarnee

Meat Curry

Makes 4 servings

Ingredients:

4 medium potatoes

2 onions

500 g (1¼ lb) goulash meat
(veal or beef)

3 tbs oil

½ tsp turmeric

3 tbs tomato purée

3 large garlic cloves, crushed

1 tsp coriander

¼ tsp cumin

½ tsp ginger

1 tsp salt

½ tsp pepper

1 pinch cardamom

1 pinch cloves

1 pinch cinnamon

½ cup water

2 tbs vinegar

1 tsp sugar

Garnish:

3 tbs chopped fresh
coriander or parsley

Directions:

Heat the oil in a large pot. Peel potatoes, cut into wedges and fry in heated oil. Do not overcook. Remove potatoes and drain on paper.

Peel and dice onions; fry in oil. Cut meat into small cubes; add to onion. Add turmeric and stir well.

Mix tomato purée, garlic, coriander, cumin, ginger, salt, pepper, cardamom, cloves, cinnamon and water in a bowl and add to pot with meat. Stir well.

Reduce heat and let simmer until meat is very tender.

Whisk together the vinegar and sugar, pour into pot and cook another 10 minutes. Garnish with coriander or parsley.

Serve with a side dish of white rice.

Lal Kuba

Meatballs with Beets

Serves 6

MEAT

Ingredients:
Sauce:
2 tbs oil
1 onion
About 300 g (12 oz) goulash
  meat (or any other meat,
  cut in chunks)
4 beets
4 crisp celery stalks
3 ripe tomatoes
2 tbs tomato purée
½ tsp salt
½ tbs sugar
Juice of 1 lemon

Meatballs:
300 g (12 oz) ground meat
  (veal or beef)
3 onions
1 tbs chopped celery leaves
½ tsp turmeric
1 egg
½ tsp pepper
½ tsp salt
1 pinch ground cloves
¼ tsp cardamom
2 tbs matza meal

Lal Kuba was one of my favorite childhood meals, served every Friday in our home in Bombay. Coming home from school, we could smell the aroma as we reached the staircase of our building. This was a sign that Shabbat was approaching – to be welcomed by a delicious family meal.

Directions:
Sauce:
Peel and cut the beets into thin slices. Peel and chop the onion. Cut the meat into bite-sized cubes. Cut the celery stalks into thin slices, and the tomatoes into wedges.

When all ingredients are ready, heat oil in a large pot. Add the meat and onion, stir and brown slightly. Then add beets, celery and tomatoes.

Stir well again; it is important that the ingredients be well blended!

Add 1½ cups water, cover pot and let simmer while preparing the meatballs. Make sure to check this sauce periodically while it cooks, adding a little more cold water, if needed.

Meatballs:
Grate onions on coarse side of grater, drain and discard the liquid. Add spices and mix well. Add the chopped meat, matza meal and egg. Stir batter until smooth. Moisten hands and roll this mixture into small meatballs.

Test to see when beets are tender, then mix lemon juice, sugar and salt together and pour into the pot of sauce.

Drop meatballs gently into the boiling sauce, one at a time, and cook until done (approx. 15 minutes).

Serve with white rice or rice pilaf.

Other Kuba dishes are found on pages 90 and 91.

Almond Chicken

Makes 4 servings

MEAT

Ingredients:

1-1½ kg (2-3 lbs) chicken –
  cut into individual
  portions
1 tsp salt
½ tsp pepper
2 tbs lemon juice
1 tbs sugar
3 tbs parve margarine
1 cup celery stalks (chopped
  into thin sticks)
2 carrots, cut into thin sticks
½ cup chicken broth or
  chicken bouillon
1 tbs cornstarch
3 tbs soy sauce
½ cup almonds–blanched,
  peeled and lightly roasted
  in very little oil
½ cup green peas (fresh or
  frozen)

Directions:

Mix salt, pepper, lemon juice and sugar. Coat the chicken pieces.

Heat margarine in large pot and sauté chicken until golden brown.

Add vegetables and stir a few minutes.

Pour in chicken broth, cover and cook 20 minutes.

Mix cornstarch and soy sauce together and pour over chicken, making sure to cover all pieces with sauce.

Add peas and simmer another few minutes.

Before serving, spread almonds over top.

Serve with fluffy boiled rice.

Avocado Appetizer

Serves 4

PARVE

Ingredients:
4 ripe avocados
1 bunch alfalfa sprouts
1 red onion
1 bunch parsley
Juice of 1 lemon
½ cup olive oil
1 large clove garlic, crushed
Salt and pepper, to taste

Optional:
Red and yellow bell peppers
for garnish

Directions:
Spread the alfalfa sprouts in bottom of dish.

Cut avocados in half and remove the pits. Peel and arrange the avocados over the alfalfa with hollow side down.

Peel onion and slice thin. Spread on top of avocado.

Make a dressing of olive oil, chopped parsley, garlic, salt and pepper and pour over avocado.

Garnish:
Garnish avocado platter with thin slices of red and yellow bell peppers, if desired.

Hawaiian Chicken

Serves 4

MEAT

Ingredients:
4 tbs onion soup mix
1½ kg (2-3 lbs) chicken
4 tbs pineapple jam or
orange marmalade
1 cup French dressing

Variation:
500 g (1 lb) frozen green beans can be added to this dish.

Directions:
Mix onion soup with 1 cup water and pour into oven-proof dish or casserole.

Cut chicken into 4 or 8 pieces and arrange on top. Brush chicken with marmalade or jam.

Pour French dressing over chicken.

Bake uncovered in oven at 180°C-200°C (350°F–400°F) for 1 hour.

Serve with light and fluffy rice.

MEAT

Hamin

Shabbat Casserole

Serves 8

Ingredients:

1½ kg (2-3 lbs) chicken
2 tbs oil
2 onions
Salt and pepper
1 tsp turmeric
2 tsp cardamom
½ cup tomato purée
3 cups rice

Optional:

1 cup white beans, soaked
*   overnight*
4 eggs

Directions:

Cut chicken into individual portions. Cut away and dice the fat for frying. Heat fat and oil in a large pan. Add the chicken and the chopped onion, and fry until golden. Mix in the turmeric, salt, pepper, cardamom and tomato purée. Stir well.

Pour in 1½ liters (6 cups) water and bring to a boil. Rinse the rice. Add rice (and white beans, if desired). Cover pot and cook 10 minutes. Wash eggs and carefully place them (whole – in shells) on the top of the casserole.

Before Shabbat, set the tightly closed pot either on a warming plate or in a warm oven 80°C-100°C (150°F–200°F). Leave overnight – until the Shabbat morning meal.

Prepared on Friday, Hamin is the traditional Shabbat meal in many Jewish homes throughout the world. It is very similar to the cholent casserole common in Eastern European Jewish cuisine.

Hamin is very filling. The dish can be varied in many ways, according to taste. Some use white beans, chick peas or bulghur (cracked wheat) to add body to this one-pot meal. Some like the dish with meat and others with poultry or large meatballs. The eggs cook in the dish all night and reach a rich, brown color when done.

Especially in the cold winter months, it is a treat to come home from Saturday services to the aroma of this special Shabbat meal.

Chocolate Mousse

Serves 4

PARVE

Ingredients:
125 g (5 oz) rich, dark
  chocolate (parve)
4 eggs
1 tbs brandy

Optional:
4 canned pears or 4 kiwi
  fruit

Garnish:
Blanched almonds or sliced
  fruit

*A double boiler is used
whenever heating
chocolate, as well as for
many sauces which might
otherwise stick to the pan.
You can make a double
boiler out of any two pots
or saucepans in your
kitchen, by nesting one
above the other. The bottom
pot is used to boil water,
while the upper one is used
to heat the chocolate, or
sauce above the water.*

Directions:
Break the chocolate into small pieces and melt it in a double boiler. Remove the melted chocolate from the heat.

Add egg yolks one at a time and stir well with a wooden spoon after each yolk is added. Add brandy and stir well.

Whip egg whites until stiff and fold carefully into the chocolate mixture until even in color.

Place ½ pear or peeled kiwi in bottom of a parfait glass or custard cup and pour chocolate mousse on top.

Add garnish.

Refrigerate at least 2 hours before serving.

PARVE

Ruth's London Tea Cake

1 cake (about 10-12 portions)

Ingredients:
2 cups light raisins
1 cup cold strong tea
1 cup sugar
2¾ cups flour
1 tsp baking powder
2 tbs orange marmalade
2 eggs

A typical "Five O'Clock Tea" cake, best served with a good cup of English tea! This cake can also be sliced like a dessert bread and served with butter.

Directions:
Soften raisins in tea and sugar overnight, or set in hot tea for 15 minutes and then let cool.

Mix flour with baking powder and stir in the tea. Stir in the orange marmalade. Then beat in the eggs, one at a time.

Pour batter into a well-greased loaf pan.

Bake at 175°C (350°F) for about 50 minutes.

Yeast Roulade

Yields 4 rolls

PARVE

Ingredients:
50 g (2 oz) yeast
1½ cups lukewarm water
1 cup melted parve
  margarine
1 pinch salt
1 cup sugar
3 egg yolks
6 cups flour

Filling:
¼ cup oil
4 tbs cocoa
¼ cup bread crumbs

Glaze:
Crystallized sugar
1 egg

DAIRY

Variation:
Butter and lukewarm milk
may be substituted for the
margarine and water.

Directions:
Crumble the yeast into the water. Add margarine, salt, sugar and egg yolks. Add flour, a little at a time.

Knead dough until smooth and elastic in consistency. Cover and leave in a cool place for 10 hours.

Divide the dough into 4 portions and roll portions into ropes. Roll out each rope on a board and flatten into a sheet until about ½ cm (¼ inch) thick.

Brush with oil and sprinkle with 1 tbs cocoa and 2 tbs bread crumbs.

Roll to a roulade (jelly roll) shape and place on baking sheet over baking paper, seam side down.

Brush with whisked egg and sprinkle with crystallized sugar.

Bake 25 minutes in 220°C (400°F) oven.

PARVE

Ashkelon Sponge Cake
Makes one 10" cake

Ingredients:
6 eggs, separated
1 cup sugar
1 tsp baking powder
1 lemon (juice and rind)
1 tbs oil
6 tbs flour
2 cups fruit purée

Garnish:
Melted chocolate
Fresh fruit, sliced

Directions:
Whip egg yolks and ½ cup sugar until light and fluffy. Add oil, juice of ½ lemon and rind of 1 lemon (grated on the small side of a grater) and whip again.

Whip egg whites separately, adding ½ cup sugar a little at a time. Add yolks to the whites.

Mix flour and baking powder and fold gently into the whipped eggs.

Pour into greased springform pan and bake ½ hour at 200°C (400°F).

After the cake cools fully, slice the cake into 2 layers and spread fruit purée between the layers.

Frost with melted chocolate and decorate with fruit.

I had my first taste of Middle Eastern cooking in Ashkelon – my first home in Israel. Ashkelon - biblical home of Samson and Delilah, boasts miles and miles of beach along Israel's Mediterranean coast, about 50 miles south of Tel Aviv. The city is a melting pot for Israelis from many different countries – each with their own delicious traditions and cuisines. Since Ashkelon is where my mother lives, thoughts of the city fill me with warm and delicious memories – some of them exotic and new, others as old and familiar as my mother's Bombay kitchen.

"Say to the people of Israel: In the seventh month on the first day of the month, you shall observe a day of solemn rest, a memorial proclaimed with trumpet blasts..."
Leviticus, Chapter 23, Verse 24

Rosh Hashanah

Rosh Hashanah, "The Head of the Year", marks the Jewish New Year. It falls during Tishrei, the seventh month of the Jewish calendar, and, according to tradition, is the anniversary of the world's creation which is said to have occurred in the year 3,760 B.C.E.

Rosh Hashanah lasts two days and is considered "one long day". The holiday has several names, all of which are used in the Bible:

Yom Teruah: The day on which the ram's horn is blown

Yom Hadin: Judgment Day

Yom Hazikaron: The Day of Remembrance

Of the four names, Rosh Hashanah is used most often, but each name describes one aspect of the holiday. It is a time to search our souls and to consider the deeds, both good and bad, which we have done during the past year, and to think about how to avoid doing negative things in the future.

Rosh Hashanah is a solemn day, but also one of thanksgiving, as we may have overcome illness and pain, and the hope of a better year to come lights the spark of happiness in us.

The ***Shofar*** is a ram's horn – the world's oldest wind instrument. The Bible mentions it in several places. At Rosh Hashana, the Shofar is blown in the synagogue, and it is believed that listening to its warm, strong tone will appeal to one's conscience and remind us of the world's Creator, as the strong tones are present but cannot be seen or touched.

The **traditional foods** of Rosh Hashanah express the nature of the holiday. The bread is baked round to symbolize a perfect coming year. People customarily dip the bread in honey instead of salt, as is done on other days. Apples and honey are eaten on the New Year with a special wish for a sweet New Year. Vegetables such as pumpkin, leeks, beets and spinach are served as symbols of growth and fruitfulness.

Dates are eaten because of their sweetness. Pomegranates are also eaten for several reasons. One is that we wish that our good deeds will be as plentiful as the pomegranate's seeds. The pomegranate is also mentioned in the Torah as a symbol for the Land of Israel. Some have associated the number of seeds found in a pomegranate with Judaism's 613 commandments.

Round Challah

Makes 4 small loaves

PARVE

Ingredients:
50 g (2 oz) yeast
2 cups lukewarm water
2 eggs
1 tbs salt
3 tbs oil
4 tbs sugar
Approx. 1 kg (2 lbs) flour

Optional:
One handful raisins

Garnish:
½ egg to brush on top
1 tsp poppyseeds

> **Challah**
> *This is the well known bread served on Shabbat. When prepared for Rosh Hashanah, it is baked in a round shape and made with extra egg and sugar, and often with raisins, to symbolize the hope for a sweet and perfect New Year.*

Directions:
Dissolve the yeast in lukewarm water and add the other ingredients, adding the flour only a little bit at a time, as the amount needed may vary. When the mixture is smooth, and the dough does not stick to the sides of the bowl, you've reached the right consistency.

Knead well and place the dough in an bowl greased with oil and cover with a damp cloth.

Let rise in a warm room for 30-40 minutes.

Lightly knead the dough again on a floured board.

Divide into 4 equal parts and roll each part into a long rope. Separate each of the 4 ropes into 3 parts, roll these out and then braid them together into one long braid. Twist each braid in a circle, in a snailshell shape. When done, you will have 4 round challah loaves, each braided as illustrated below.

Place the 4 loaves on a paper-covered baking sheet; cover with cloth and let rise about 25 minutes while oven preheats to 220°C (425°F).

Brush each with beaten egg and sprinkle with poppyseeds, before putting in oven.

Bake at 425°F about 35 minutes, until golden brown.

Great Grandma's Salad
Serves 4

PARVE

Ingredients:
1 cup canned beets, sliced thin

2 cups peeled Granny Smith apples, sliced thin (Note: any tart apples may be used)

2 cups cooked celery root, cut into cubes

3-4 tbs mayonnaise

Garnish:
Watercress

2 hard-boiled eggs

Directions:
Combine all 3 items with a little mayonnaise and some of the juice from the beets. Garnish with watercress and the wedges of hard-boiled egg.

Serving Suggestion:
Since this salad is parve, it can accompany any dish and goes very well with both fish and meat.

This salad makes an excellent light meal when combined with smoked turkey breast, available from any kosher butcher.

My husband's great grandmother came from a long line of artists. Perhaps because of the aesthetic sense which had been instilled in her family for generations, she had a very keen eye for colors. This particularly colorful salad remained one of her favorites until the day she died – at the age of 99 !

MEAT

Chicken in
Honey Mustard Sauce
Serves 6

Ingredients:
1½-2 kg (3-4 lbs) large
  chicken
½ cup flour
½ tsp grated nutmeg
½ tsp ginger
½ tsp cloves
½ tsp salt
4 tbs parve margarine
½ cup Dijon mustard
½ cup honey
½ cup chicken bouillon

Garnish:
Blanched roasted almonds

Directions:
Cut the chicken into individual-sized portions.

Mix the flour with the spices and coat each piece of chicken. Brown the chicken in the melted margarine.

Arrange the chicken in a greased pan.

Mix the honey, mustard and bouillon and pour this over the chicken pieces.

Cover and bake in preheated 200°C (375°F) oven for about 45 minutes.

Garnish with the roasted almonds and serve over a bed of white rice.

Sweetness and good health are two of the most traditional wishes made for the New Year. This dish should help contribute to both!

Carrots à l'Orange

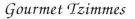

Gourmet Tzimmes

Serves 8

PARVE

Ingredients:
1 kg (2 lbs) carrots
1 cup orange juice
1 tbs sugar
½ tsp salt
½ tsp ginger
1 tbs parve margarine
2 tbs cornstarch
¼ cup water

Garnish:
Mint leaves and/or thin
  slices of orange

Directions:
Wash and peel the carrots and cut in 1-inch slices or in long sticks, like french fries.

Melt margarine in a pot and add carrots. Stir. In another pot, add sugar, salt and ginger to the orange juice. Boil this juice mixture for 15-20 minutes.

Spoon carrots onto serving platter and keep warm.

Stir together: cornstarch and water and pour into the boiling orange juice mixture. Stir well, until sauce is smooth; simmer another 3 minutes.

Pour sauce over carrots. Garnish with mint leaves and/or thin slices of orange. Serve.

> *Tzimmes **is a favorite side dish in which carrots are cooked in sugar and water. There are many versions of this recipe "just like mother used to make". But here is one version with a little more flavor – "like my mother never made it"! I think it has a fresh taste – and it's a great way to wish each one at the table a sweet New Year.***

Israeli Honey Cake

Makes 1 large cake

Ingredients:

1 cup fresh-squeezed orange
   juice
1 cup honey
1 cup very strong coffee
4 eggs
2 tbs salad oil
1 cup sugar
4 cups flour
¼ tsp salt
1 tsp cinnamon
½ tsp cloves
½ tsp cardamom
2 tsp baking powder
1 tsp baking soda

Directions:

Combine the orange juice, honey and coffee in a mixing bowl. In another bowl, beat the eggs until light and fluffy, then add the oil gradually. Combine all the dry ingredients and add to the eggs, alternating with the liquid mixture. Beat this to a smooth batter.

Pour into a greased 28 cm (11") baking pan and bake at 170°C (350°F) for about 50 minutes.

> *Apples and honey . . . At this time of year, just about every Jewish home is filled with the aroma of spices as a honey cake bakes in the oven. And the variety of apples available in early autumn make apple pies, cakes and strudels common New Year's desserts.*

"Berry Special" Apple Pie

1 pie, serves 8

Ingredients:
Dough:
2 cups flour
¾ cup parve margarine
½ cup sugar
1 egg

Filling:
1 kg (2 lbs) Granny Smith
   apples
1 tsp vanilla
1-2 tbs sugar
4 tbs raspberry jam
4 tbs bread crumbs (or matza
   meal)

For Topping:
Crystallized sugar, egg

Directions:

Be sure all ingredients are chilled. Crumble together: flour, margarine and sugar. Then add the egg. Chill dough for 30 minutes. Meanwhile, peel and core the apples, and slice into thin wedges.

Press ⅔ of the dough onto bottom and sides of a non-greased springform cake pan. Spread raspberry jam over the dough and arrange a mixture of apple wedges, vanilla, sugar and bread crumbs on top.

Roll the remaining dough into long thin strips and lattice them over the cake. Brush with beaten egg and sprinkle with crystallized sugar.

Bake at 200°C (375°F) for about 45 minutes, until golden-brown.

> "On the tenth day of this seventh month is the Day of Atonement; it shall be a holy gathering for you, and you shall afflict yourselves and present an offering by fire to the Lord. And you shall do no work on this day, for it is a day of atonement for you before the Lord your God."
>
> Leviticus, Chapter 23, Verses 27-28

Yom Kippur

The days from Rosh Hashanah to *Yom Kippur*, the Day of Atonement, are called the **10 days of penance**, when we, through good deeds, prayer and repentance, can soften a possibly bad fate.

Yom Kippur is, together with Shabbat, the holiest day of the Jewish year. Yom Kippur, which starts on the 9th day of Tishrei in the evening and ends 25 hours later, is a day of fasting. All healthy adults are expected to fast, including boys over the age of 13 and girls from age 12. During the fast, all food and drink are forbidden – not even a drop of water is to be swallowed.

The **pre-fast meal** is eaten in the early evening and should end one hour before sundown. It is wise to abstain from heavily seasoned and salted food, as these foods can increase one's thirst and appetite.

A light chicken soup with Kreplach (stuffed dumplings) is traditional in many homes. Cooked poultry, potatoes or rice, fresh fruit and a glass of seltzer are what I serve my family.

After a day of prayer and introspection, the **end of the fast** is marked the next evening with the blowing of the Shofar at the *Neila* (closing) prayer service in the synagogue. That's when Heaven's gate is considered closed, sealing our fate for the new year. With hope in our hearts, and relief at once again having survived the fast, we head home to share a light meal with our families.

While the meal (made the previous day) is being heated, we usually start with a cup of tea and a piece of cake (see Nanna's Rings and Filled Crescents). Again, my menu at home is a light one: chicken soup, cooked poultry, salad and lots of seltzer and fresh fruit.

Kreplach
Savory Dumplings
Serves 6-8

Ingredients:
Filling:
1 cup ground veal, beef or
   chicken
2 tbs parve margarine
1 onion
Salt and pepper

Dough:
1 cup flour
½ tsp baking powder
1 egg yolk
¼ cup water
½ tsp salt

---

*Kreplach is usually served
in soup. It is a tradition to
serve kreplach before the
Yom Kippur fast, as well as
on the last day of Sukkoth
and on Purim. The tiny
sealed pockets of dough are
to symbolize protection
from hardship during the
coming year. The
traditional meat filling can
be varied with ground
chicken breast, liver, or a
vegetable filling.*

Directions:
Filling:
(The filling is made first and left to cool while preparing the dough.)

Chop onion very fine. Melt margarine in pan and stir in onion, meat, salt and pepper.

Cook, stirring continuously until done, about 5-6 minutes.

Let cool.

Dough:
Combine flour and baking powder in a large bowl and make a hollow in the middle. Add the remaining ingredients into the hollow and knead to a smooth dough. Roll the dough as thin as possible on a floured board and cut into 5 cm (2½") squares.

Place a small teaspoonful of the filling on each square and fold the corners to make a triangle. Press closed, sealing the sides.

Fill a large pan with 2 liters (2 quarts) of water and 1 tbs salt; bring to boil. Add the kreplach triangles a few at a time. Let cook until they float to the surface.

Remove the kreplach from the water with a slotted spoon; keep dry and cool.

Serve in hot soup.

As a variation, kreplach may also be fried and served as a side dish.

Kreplach

Savory Dumplings

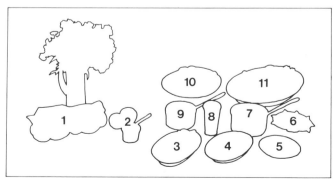

Rosh Hashanah and Yom Kippur

PARVE

Nanna's Rings and Filled Crescents

Makes 70-80 pastries

Ingredients:

Dough:
2 cups melted parve margarine
1½ cups water
1½ tbs baking powder
1 kg (2 lbs) flour
4 tbs sugar
1 tsp salt
1 tsp cardamom
1 tsp ground fennel seed

Filling No. 1:
1 cup shredded coconut
¼ cup sugar
1 tsp cardamom
1 egg white
Chopped nuts (optional)
1 tsp rosewater (usually available at your pharmacy)

Filling No. 2:
1 cup chopped nuts
2-3 tbs mashed figs or dates
1 tsp vanilla or cardamom

Directions for Dough:
Melt margarine, cool and mix with water. Combine dry ingredients in large bowl and make a hollow in the middle. Add the liquids and knead until completely blended. Form into ball, cover and let stand in a cool place for ½ hour. Divide dough into walnut-sized balls.

For Nanna's Rings:
Roll each dough ball into a thin strip about 15 cm (6 inches) long and join the ends to form a ring.

For Filled Crescents:
Press balls to form a flat circle about 10 cm (4 inches) in diameter. Spoon 1 tbs of filling on ½ of the circle, fold other half over the top and press edges together to seal.

Place the rings and crescents on baking pan covered with baking paper and bake about 20 minutes at 200°C (375°F) until light and golden. If desired, brush with beaten egg before baking to form a glaze.

DAIRY

Alternate Filling:
100 g (4 oz) cream cheese
100g (4oz) grated cheese (use a mild yellow cheese)
1 egg yolk
1 tbs bread crumbs

"And Abraham hastened into the tent to Sarah, and said, 'Make ready quickly three measures of fine meal, knead it and make cakes.'"

Genesis, Chapter 18, Verse 6

*"...On the fifteenth day of this seventh month and for seven days is the
Feast of Booths to the Lord."*
Leviticus, Chapter 23, Verse 34

*"In order that your generations will know that I made the people of Israel dwell in
booths when I brought them out of the land of Egypt: I am the Lord your God."*
Leviticus, Chapter 23, Verse 43

Sukkoth

The ten days of penance which started with Rosh Hashanah and ended with Yom Kippur are now over. *Sukkoth*, also called, *"Zman Simchtenu"* – the time of our joy – now begins.

"You shall feel joy at your feast", is an obligation on Sukkoth, and this is something we should take to heart. It is traditional to build a *sukka* – a booth with a loosely-thatched roof – outside of one's home. This booth is a symbol of God's protection. The sukka also symbolizes the often dangerous wanderings of our forefathers through the desert on their way from slavery to freedom. On their way, they lived in these temporary shelters.

The construction of the sukka should be started as soon as Yom Kippur ends. The booth consists of four walls, made of canvas, wood, or other material. The roof is made of branches and/or leaves – thatched loosely so that one may glimpse the stars in the sky above. The sukka is decorated with flowers, fruit and other colorful decorations.

Jews are called upon to eat their meals in the sukka during this holiday. Thus the sukka becomes a colorful gathering place for the family's holiday meals.

The holiday of Sukkoth is also a harvest festival (*"Hag Ha-asif"*) – since in Israel the harvest of grapes, olives and other crops ends at this time of year. Now one waits in hope for the first rain and the start of a new and fertile planting year.

A special combination of **four different plant species** is used at Sukkoth. It consists of three different types of branches and one fruit, the citron (*"etrog"*). The three branches are: the palm branch (*"lulav"*), myrtle (*"hadassim"*) and the willow (*"aravot"*). Every day during Sukkoth, a special prayer of thanksgiving is said. At this time, all four of these plants are held in the hand and shaken up and down and in the direction of each of the four corners of the world.

There are many different explanations given for combining these particular four plants. One is that the different qualities of each remind us that people are also different, yet must come together in order for a healthy society to function.

Also, although each of these plant species may have been prevalent in ancient Israel, they are often rare and hard to get today: especially outside of Israel.

Therefore, seeing people on their way to synagogue or to Sukkoth celebrations with these long branches and fragrant fruit in hand, becomes an undeniable sign that a special holiday has arrived.

Citrons, which were evidently fairly common in the days of the Bible, are now grown only on special farms in Israel. The citron cannot be eaten raw and since it is rare and thus very expensive, one does not often find it cooked. However, if you're lucky enough to get a few of these exotic fruits after the Sukkoth festival, you can make a delicious marmelade.

The seventh and last day of the Sukkoth feast marks the end of the Judgment period. In a special ceremony in the synagogue, the willow branches are struck against a hard surface to produce the sound of rain. It is, at the same time, the last chance to rid one of one's sins, as the leaves are falling from the branches. Now, just before judgment time is over, we pray that we may receive a mild judgment during the coming year.

The day after Sukkoth is called *Shemini Atzeret* – The Gathering on the Eighth Day. Again, prayers for rain are recited in every synagogue. The rain will bring a blessing to the coming year's harvest.

This is something which links Jewish communities throughout the world to each other, as well as to their common roots in the land of Israel.

The holiday of *Simchat Torah* falls on the next day. The name of this holiday means: Joy of the Torah. The last passage in the Torah is read in the synagogue, and immediately afterward, one starts reading the Torah again from the beginning, making an unbroken cycle of the reading of the law, as is done in every synagogue each Shabbat. In this way, we're reminded that the Torah will always be a new source of inspiration and guidance for us.

The **Torah scrolls** – with their colorfully decorated embroidered covers and shiny ornaments – are all taken out of their special cabinet, the ark. The congregation sings and dances, holding the Torah scrolls high. Children are a special part of this celebration and their joy adds to the general feeling of hope and rejoicing which mark this day. Chocolates, candies, and other treats, such as apples, are passed around. When the synagogue celebration ends, the family goes home to enjoy a very special holiday meal.

Bombay Chicken Curry with Pilaf

Serves 4

Ingredients:
1½-2 kg (3-4 lbs) chicken
½ kg (1 lb) potatoes
½ cup oil
2 onions
1 large garlic clove, crushed
1 pinch chili powder
1 tsp turmeric
1 tsp ginger
1 whole clove or
½ tsp ground cloves
Salt and pepper, to taste
1 tbs tomato purée
Juice of 1 lemon

Ingredients for Rice Pilaf:
1 onion
½ cup oil
1 tsp turmeric
1 whole clove or
½ tsp ground cloves
½ tsp cardamom
½ tsp allspice
2 cups rice
¼ cup raisins
½ cup almonds
1 tbs margarine

Directions:
Peel and wash potatoes, cut into quarters and dry on paper towels. Heat oil in pan and sautée in hot oil until golden brown. Remove potatoes from pan and add a little salt.

Chop onion and sautée in the same oil until clear. Add crushed garlic, spices, tomato purée and lemon juice. This mixture is called "massala" in India.

Cut the chicken into portions and simmer the pieces in the hot masala. Add 1 cup of water and cook on low heat, about 20 minutes.

Add potatoes and boil another 10 minutes.

Meanwhile, make the pilaf. Chop the onion and sautée in the hot oil. Add spices, rice and raisins and stir well. Immediately add 3 cups water and boil until the rice is done, about 15 minutes.

Blanch and peel almonds and sautée them in margarine. Garnish the rice pilaf with the almonds, and serve this pilaf with the chicken.

This is an inexpensive and very tasty main meal, well seasoned, as Indian food often is. The light meat of the chicken can take quite a bit of spice. However, one may eliminate the chili powder when cooking for a less adventurous palate.

Fillet of Sole Niçoise

Serves 4

DAIRY

Ingredients:

8 fish fillets: sole, plaice or
  flounder
Juice of 1 lemon
Salt and pepper to taste
½ cup bread crumbs
1 egg
2 tbs olive oil
2 onions
3 bell peppers – red, green,
  yellow
2 tomatoes
½ cup olives (black and
  green)
1 bunch fresh parsley
1 tsp oregano or thyme
½ cup white wine or
  vegetable bouillon

Garnish:

1 cup crème fraîche (see pg.
  53) or sour cream
3 tbs lemon juice
1 egg yolk

Directions:

Sprinkle lemon juice, salt and pepper over the fish
and let chill for about an hour. Pat dry, coat with egg
and bread crumbs, and fry in a little margarine 5-6
minutes on each side. Set fish aside while preparing
the sauce.

Heat the olive oil in the pan, peel and slice the
onion and sautée until clear.

Cut bell peppers into strips; add them together with
the sliced tomatoes and pitted olives. Stir gently.
Mince parsley and add together with thyme or
oregano. Salt and pepper to taste.

Arrange the vegetables in an oven-proof dish, place
the fillets on top and add wine or bouillon.

Combine crème fraîche, lemon juice and 2 tbs water.
Beat egg yolk and fold into crème fraîche and pour
over fillets.

Bake at 200°C (375°F) for about 10 minutes, until
golden brown.

PARVE

Variation:
Here's a non-dairy garnish.
Instead of crème fraîche,
try this tomato sauce:
Chopped peeled tomatoes,
lemon, ¼ tsp cayenne
pepper, salt and pepper.

Mediterranean Beet Salad

Serves 6-8

PARVE

Ingredients:
1 kg (2 lbs) beets
½ kg (1 lb) large tomatoes
1 red onion
6-7 sprigs fresh mint or
* celery leaves*
1 bunch of fresh coriander
Juice of 1 lemon
Salt to taste

Directions:
Wash the beets well. Cook unpeeled beets in covered pot of water until done. Remove from water (save this water to make beet juice, below).

Peel and cut the beets into thin slices. Slice tomatoes.

Cut onion into rings.

Arrange in layers on a serving dish. Garnish with chopped mint or celery and coriander leaves. Pour lemon juice over the salad and sprinkle with salt.

"Borscht" – Beet Juice
Cool the cooking water left from boiled beets. Add lemon juice and sugar to taste. Serve over ice in tall glass.
Garnish:
Add mint leaves on top and place a thin slice of lemon on rim of glass.

Tomato Salad

Serves 6-8

Use the same amount of tomatoes as in the beet salad, and 1 red onion. Slice ripe tomatoes and arrange on a serving dish. Top with rings of onion.

Season with salt, pepper, crushed garlic (optional), and dress with lemon juice and olive oil. Garnish with chopped parsley.

Autumn Fruit Pie

Serves 10

Ingredients for Dough:
3½ cups flour
250 g (10 oz) parve
   margarine
½ cup sugar
1 tsp vanilla
2 tsp baking powder
2 eggs
3 tbs matza meal or bread
   crumbs

Ingredients for Filling:
1 kg (2 lbs) fruit: any
   combination of plums,
   apples, peaches or apricots
2 tbs sugar

Optional:
2-3 tbs fruit preserves (black
   currant or black raspberry
   jam)

Garnish:
Egg, crystallized sugar
Chopped nuts

Directions:
Combine flour, sugar, baking powder and vanilla in large bowl. Crumble cold margarine into flour and work in the eggs. Chill this dough for 30 minutes.

Prepare the fruit: Peel and core the apples and slice into thin wedges. Remove skin from plums, apricots and peaches and cut into wedges.

Press ⅔ of the dough onto bottom and sides of a small baking pan and sprinkle with matza meal or bread crumbs. Mix fruit with sugar and arrange on top of dough in the baking pan.

Roll the remaining ⅓ of the dough flat to fit top of pan. Place over the fruit and press edges together to seal the pie on all sides. If desired, make 10-12 slits in the dough and use a pastry bag to inject the preserves into slits.

Brush the pie with beaten egg. Garnish with sugar and/or chopped nuts.

Bake at 180°C (350°F) for 45 minutes.

Tutti Frutti Ice Cream

Serves 10-12

Ingredients:
4 egg yolks
½ cup sugar
1 tsp vanilla
1 large can of fruit cocktail
½ liter (1 pint) whipping
  cream
2 egg whites
1 tsp almond oil for the
  mold

Optional:
2 oz soft milk chocolate, or
  semi-sweet chocolate

Garnish:
Fresh fruit, sliced thin

Directions:
Beat egg yolks and sugar until light and fluffy. Add vanilla, rum and chocolate (broken into small pieces). Add drained fruit cocktail.

In two separate bowls whip cream and beat egg whites until stiff. Fold the whipped cream into the egg yolk and fruit mixture and then fold in the stiffened egg whites.

Oil a springform pan or freezer mold with the almond oil and pour in the ice cream mixture.

Freeze at least 4-5 hours.

One can scoop the ice cream to serve in bowls, or serve it as an ice cream cake.

Serve garnished with fresh fruit slices.

Aunt Sus's Date Cake

Makes a 10" cake

PARVE

Ingredients:
6 eggs
¾ cup sugar
2 cups almonds
1 cup dates, dried and pitted
1 tsp baking powder
½ tsp vanilla
3 tbs matza meal

Optional:
1 tbs brandy (or other liqueur)

Garnish:
Powdered sugar
Fresh dates

Directions:
Beat egg yolks and sugar until light and fluffy. Dice almonds. Chop dates into small pieces.

Combine almonds, baking powder and vanilla and stir into eggs. Sprinkle the chopped dates with matza meal and add to the dough.

Pour in the brandy or liqueur.

Pour into a well-greased springform pan about 25 cm (10") in diameter and bake for 1 hour at 175°C (350°F).

Note: After the first ½ hour of baking, cover the cake with foil to keep it from turning too dark on top.

Our Aunt Sus used to prepare this cake for holidays throughout the year. Note that because there is no flour in this cake, it is also kosher for Passover. Just be sure to check that the ingredients used are labeled kosher for Passover.

Crème Fraîche Cake

Moist Sour Cream Cake

12-15 portions

DAIRY

Ingredients:
Dough:
3½ cups flour
2 tsp baking powder
2 tsp vanilla
1 tbs grated lemon peel
200 g (8 oz) margarine
2 eggs
½ cup sugar
½ cup milk

Cream:
6 tbs margarine
½ cup powdered sugar
1 tsp vanilla
2 egg yolks
1 tbs fruit liqueur
½ liter (2 cups) sour cream,
    or crème fraîche
400 g (1 lb) raspberries
1 cup chopped nuts

DAIRY

Variation:
**Instead of raspberries, try
using fresh blackberries,
strawberries or kiwi.
Canned fruit may also be
used.**

Directions for Dough:

Combine flour, sugar, baking powder, grated lemon peel and vanilla in bowl. Crumble the cold margarine into flour and add the eggs. Pour ½ of the dough into a greased rectangular baking pan about 45 cm (15") long.

Crumble the other half of the dough into an oven-proof dish. Put both the cake pan and the oven-proof dish into a 200°C (400°F) oven and bake for 10 minutes. (The crumbs will be used to top the cake.)

Let the crumbs cool and spoon the milk over the baked cake, letting it soak into the cake – this is the cake's bottom layer. Set aside.

Directions for Cream:

Beat margarine and sugar; add egg yolks, vanilla and fruit liqueur. Fold in the sour cream or crème fraîche. Place the berries on the moist cake (the bottom layer) and spread the cream over the berries, followed by the chopped nuts and cake crumbs. Let cool.

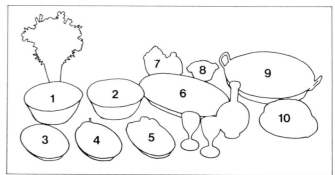

Sukkoth and Cheshvan

French Apple Pie

Serves 8

PARVE

Ingredients:
8 Granny Smith, or other
   tart apples
½ cup sugar
1 tsp vanilla
2½ cups almonds, chopped
5 tbs parve margarine
1¼ cup sugar (for almond
   batter)
Grated peel of 1 lemon
3 eggs

DAIRY

Topping Variation:
For a dairy meal, crème
fraîche, or sour cream, may
be served with the pie.

Directions:
Peel and core the apples and cut into wedges. Cook the apples in about ½ cup water until just barely soft, to make a chunky applesauce. Remove from heat and add sugar and vanilla.

Chop almonds.

Melt margarine with sugar in pan – remove from heat to cool. Add the chopped almonds, lemon peel, 2 whole eggs and 1 yolk. Beat the egg white which remains and fold into almond dough.

Pour the applesauce into an oven-proof dish and spread the almond dough on top.

Bake in a 225°C (425°F) oven until top is golden brown.

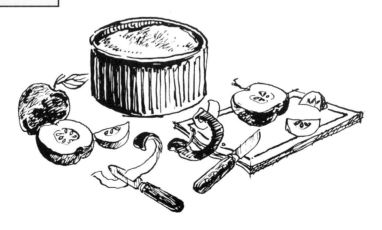

Danish Crown Cake

Serves 8

PARVE

Ingredients:
4 tbs parve margarine
1 cup sugar
4 eggs, separated
3 small, boiled potatoes
2 ½ cups almonds
A little matza meal or bread
    crumbs (to coat cake pan)

Frosting:
100 g (4 oz) semi-sweet
    chocolate (parve - not
    milk chocolate)
2 tbs parve margarine
Kiwi or other fresh fruit

*This recipe is a variation of
"the Crown Cake", an old
favorite of the Danish
Jewish community. The
cake is also suitable for
Passover, if the bread
crumbs are omitted.*

Directions:
Beat the margarine and sugar until light and fluffy. Add the egg yolks one at a time, beating very well.

Chop the almonds, and mash the potatoes with a fork. Combine the almonds and potatoes and add them into the sugar and margarine mixture. Whip the egg whites until stiff and fold into the batter.

Grease a springform cake pan with margarine and sprinkle the inside of pan (bottom and sides) with matza meal or bread crumbs to prevent cake from sticking. Pour in batter.

Bake in a preheated oven at 200°C (400°F) for 45 minutes. Cool.

Frosting:
Melt the chocolate and margarine in a double boiler. Pour this chocolate mixture over the the cooled cake, spreading it evenly on the top and sides.

Decorate with slices of kiwi or other fruit.

Liver Pâté

Serves 8

Ingredients:

500 g (2 lbs) veal liver
1 onion
½ cup melted parve
  margarine
½ cup chicken fat
3 tbs flour
1 cup bouillon
3 eggs
1 tsp salt
1 tsp pepper

---

*Place the mold or baking
dish into a large oven pan
and add enough water to
reach half the height of the
pan, so that the mold or
inner dish is surrounded by
liquid.
Place the baking pan on the
lowest shelf in the oven.
This method is often used
for paté.*

---

*The Autumn month of
Cheshvan has no particular
Jewish holiday.
The recipes on the following
pages are suitable as
everyday dishes.*

Directions:

In a food processor or blender, blend the onions and liver until smooth.

Melt the margarine and chicken fat in a saucepan.

Remove the pan from the burner and stir in the flour with swift strokes.

Add the bouillon, return to the burner and allow to simmer while stirring well, for 2-3 minutes.

Remove pot from heat and add the ground liver and onion, together with the eggs and spices. Mix well.

Pour into a well-greased mold and cover. Place in a pan of water (see box).

Bake at 200°C (400°F) for one hour.

MEAT

Mother's Delicious Meat Patties
Serves 6

Ingredients:

2 pieces of matza or 2 slices
   of white bread
3 onions
½ tsp turmeric
½ tsp cardamom
½ cup celery, chopped
1 tsp ground coriander
1 pinch ground cloves
1 tsp ground ginger
4 cloves of garlic
1 egg
1 tsp salt
500 g (1 lb) ground veal
4 tbs matza meal or bread
   crumbs for coating
Oil for frying

Directions:

Soak the matza or bread in water for about 10 minutes.

Peel and grate the onion and press out the liquid. Add all spices. Squeeze the water from the soaked bread or matza. Crumble the bread or matza and mix with onion and spices.

Add the ground meat and egg. Mix all the ingredients together well.

Form small flat patties with moistened hands to avoid sticking.

Coat them with matza meal or bread crumbs and fry in hot oil.

MEAT

Batana Kuba

Meatballs in Spicy Green Pea Sauce

Serves 4-6

Ingredients:

1 onion
2 tbs oil
1 cup water
2 tsp ground coriander
1 tsp ground cumin
¼ tsp turmeric
½ tsp chili or cayenne
  powder
1 tsp ground ginger
2 cloves of garlic
6 curry or bay leaves
1 tsp salt
½ cup tomato paste
500 g (1 lb) frozen green
  peas

Ingredients for meatballs:

300 g (¾ lb) ground veal
3 onions, chopped
1 tbs celery or mint, chopped
½ tsp turmeric
½ tsp pepper
½ tsp salt
1 pinch ground cloves
¼ tsp cardamom
2 tbs matza or bread crumbs
1 egg

Directions:

Peel and finely chop onion. Fry until golden in hot oil.

Add half of the water and allow onion to simmer for 3-4 minutes.

Add spices and stir well, and let simmer for 4-5 minutes. Then add tomato paste and the other half of the water.

Allow again to simmer for 5 minutes, before adding the green peas. Bring to boil then return to simmer.

Combine all ingredients for meatballs.

Form small meatballs and drop them a couple at a time into the boiling sauce.

Cover pot and allow to boil for about 15 minutes or until meatballs are cooked. If necessary, add more water.

Serve with boiled white rice.

For another way to prepare these meatballs, see the other Kuba recipes on pages 90-91.

Rachel's Fish Curry

Serves 4

PARVE

Ingredients:
2 tbs oil
1 large onion
½ tsp cumin
2 tsp coriander powder
½ tsp chili or cayenne
  powder
½ tsp turmeric
1 tsp salt
½ tsp garam massala*
2 cloves garlic, crushed
1 tsp ground ginger
1 cup grated tomatoes
1 big or 2 small eggplants
1 kg (2 lbs) codfish fillets
1 tbs coconut cream*
Juice of 1 lemon

Garnish:
Fresh coriander or parsley

* See page 184

Directions:
Heat the oil in a medium size pot.

Peel and dice the onion and fry it until golden in color.

Combine coriander, cumin, turmeric, salt, garam massala, garlic and ginger in about ½ cup water and add it to the onion, stirring it gently – allow to simmer for 5-6 minutes and then add tomato purée.

Wash and dice the eggplant and add it to the sauce. Add about ¼-½ cup water and stir very well.

Allow to cook for about 15 minutes.

Cut the fish into small pieces and carefully add them to the sauce and continue simmering for 10 minutes.

Add the coconut cream and lemon, and sprinkle chopped fresh coriander or parsley on top as a garnish.

Serve hot with white rice.

This is my favorite fish curry, prepared by my sister-in-law, Rachel, in her Bombay kitchen. It's also suited for the non-Indian palate. Serve with a good portion of white boiled rice.

MEAT

Paëlla

Spanish Rice with Chicken

Serves 4-6

Ingredients:

1 kg (2 1bs) chicken
2 cups rice
100 g (3 oz) parve margarine
½ cup olive oil
1 small onion
1 red bell pepper
1 green bell pepper
2 tomatoes
2 cloves of garlic
3 cups chicken broth (made
   with the bones of the
   chicken)
Salt and pepper to taste
1 tsp turmeric (or saffron, if
   available)
½ tsp cayenne pepper
2 bay leaves
½ tsp curry powder
2 tbs capers
2 tbs chopped parsley
20 olives, both black and
   green (pitted)

Optional: 8-10 artichoke
   hearts (from a tin or frozen)

> Paëlla means a pan.
> Paella is a Spanish meal
> usually prepared in a big
> round pan with handles at the
> sides.
> It can also be prepared in a
> pot and later arranged in a
> big heat-proof dish.
> There are many ways to
> experiment with paëlla by
> changing the vegetables, or
> meat that you use. Let your
> taste and creativity guide you.

Directions:

Cut the chicken off the bone in 8 small portions and use the rest to make the broth called for later on.

Sprinkle salt and pepper on the chicken pieces and fry them golden in margarine in a pan.

Peel and dice onion and garlic, cut the peppers in sticks, blanch and peel tomatoes and cut them in slices.

Heat the olive oil in a big pot, add the onion and garlic, put in the rice and stir a minute, add the spices and chicken pieces and stir very well.

Pour 3 cups chicken broth into the pot.

Add the pepper sticks and olives and allow the dish to simmer for 30 minutes.

Arrange in serving dish, garnish with capers, parsley and artichoke hearts.

Keep the paëlla warm in the oven, covered, until ready to be served.

Serve with French bread and a tomato salad.

(See front cover photo).

Tabouli

Bulghur Salad

Serves 4-6

PARVE

Ingredients:
2 cups parboiled bulghur
1 liter (4 cups) water
1 medium onion
6 tbs chopped parsley
3 tbs of different greens:
   scallion, mint leaves, fresh
   dill, etc.
½ cup olive oil
Juice of 2 lemons
½ cup black olives
1 green bell pepper
2 tomatoes

Optional:
Cucumber pickled in brine

Bulghur is precooked crushed wheat. When cooked in bouillon and spices, it can be used as a substitute for rice, or other side dishes.
Bulghur cooks in 10 min. Check directions for preparing on package.
I can recommend bulghur as a tasty and filling salad, when spiced with a fresh dressing.

Directions:
Soak the parboiled bulghur in water for one hour.

Strain the bulghur and spread it on a dish towel.

Roll the towel like a roulade and wring out the remaining water.

Put the bulghur in a big bowl.

Chop the onions and peppers very fine and mix them in. Do the same if pickled cucumbers are used.

Remove the pits from the olives and cut them in very small pieces, keep a few whole to garnish.

Mix the rest of the ingredients in a bowl.

Mix the lemon juice, olive oil, salt and pepper together and pour the dressing over the salad.

Garnish with tomato wedges and black olives.

MEAT

Hari Kebab

Meatballs in Green Curry

Serves 4

Ingredients:
Massala:
3 cloves of garlic
1 small piece of fresh ginger
*   or 1 tsp ginger powder*
2 tbs fresh coriander
4 green bell peppers

Meatballs:
500 g (1 lb) ground meat
1 onion, grated
1 tsb salt
1 tsp pepper
1 tbs of the massala

Sauce:
3 tbs oil
4 medium potatoes
2 onions
2 grated tomatoes
½ tsp turmeric
½ tsp salt
½ tsp white pepper
¾ cup water

Directions:
Peel the garlic and the fresh ginger. Remove stem and seeds from the peppers.

Chop the garlic, ginger, peppers and coriander in a blender or food processor.

Combine the minced meat, grated onion, salt, pepper and one tablespoon of massala.

Form meatballs and keep them cold, while the sauce is prepared.

Heat the oil in a pot.

Peel the potatoes and cut into wedges. Fry them until golden brown in the warm oil. Remove them onto absorbent paper.

Peel and dice the onion and sautée lightly in the oil. Add the turmeric, salt and pepper and stir well.

Pour the massala and tomatoes in while stirring well.

Add ¾ cup water. When the sauce boils, put in the meatballs, a few at a time.

Allow to simmer for 10-15 minutes.

Add potatoes and allow to simmer for 10-15 more minutes.

> *These meatballs taste and smell especially delicious when fresh ingredients are used.*
> *They are good with rice, mashed potatoes or pasta.*

"We light these candles to remind us of the miracles, the wonders, the salvations and the battles that You have carried out for our forefathers in those days, at this season, through Your holy priests."
Hymn said upon the lighting of the Hannukah candles

Hannukah

The Hebrew word **Hannukah** means consecration. The holiday commemorates the revival and new consecration of the ancient Temple in the year 165 B.C.E., following the Maccabean rebellion. The celebration is also called *Hag HaOrot*, the Feast of Lights, because of the candles which are lit on each of the eight nights of the holiday.

Hannukah begins on the 25th of Kislev in the Hebrew calendar, which usually falls in the middle of December.

The events which are celebrated on Hannukah took place 1,000 years after the death of Moses. They are chronicled in the two ancient books of the Maccabees – and not in the Bible itself. **The Hannukah story** tells of the struggle of the ancient Jewish people to maintain their distinctive identity and religion in the face of Greek culture which threatened to engulf them.

Because Hannukah is not a Biblical holiday, it does not carry restrictions on work or travel.

The Hannukah Story: In the years 175-163 B.C.E., the ancient Greek empire dominated the Middle East, including Syria, where **King Antiochus the IVth** ruled on behalf of the Greeks. Antiochus conquered Jerusalem in the year 168 B.C.E. and forced the Jews of ancient Israel to embrace Hellenistic culture and to worship Greek gods. He forbade the practice of the Jewish religion. While some Jews adapted to the Greek culture, others resisted, clinging to Jewish ways.

Antiochus and his Syrian army plundered the **Jewish Temple** and desecrated it by erecting a statue of the Greek god, Zeus, inside the Temple.

Antiochus demanded that the Jews bow before the statue.

Those who refused were brutally killed. Many fled and lived in fear, hiding in caves. Others pretended to be converts to Hellenism, adopting Greek clothing and habits, while remaining secret believers in the Jewish religion.

The brutality of Antiochus sparked a revolutionary fire in the hearts of a small group of brave men, led by the Hashmonean priest, Mattathius, and his five sons. Mattathius was zealous and brave but very old. Soon, one of his sons, Judah, took over leadership of the rebels. Judah became known as the Maccabee, a name which comes from the Hebrew word to strike. The rebels called themselves the **Maccabees**.

Despite the fact that the Jews were greatly outnumbered by the Syrians, the rebellion grew from a handful of fighters to a network of rebels throughout conquered Israel. Judah's guerrilla tactics of surprise attacks won many battles in the countryside.

They fought in Jerusalem and conquered the part of the city the Temple was in. The desecrated Temple was cleansed and purified and the Jewish Hellenists fled to Syria.

On the 25th day of Kislev, 165 B.C.E., the Temple was rededicated. Before the **consecration ceremony**, the priests searched for pure oil to light the great Temple menorah, but found only one tiny jug – with enough oil for one day. The story tells us that this oil lasted for eight days, giving the priests enough time to prepare new oil. This is the reason that Hannukah, the Hebrew word for consecration, is celebrated for eight days. The *Menorah,* or *Hannukiah,* is lit.

The **Menorah** holds nine candles: one for each of the eight nights, and an additional candle, used to light the others. One candle is lit on the first night of Hannukah, two on the second night, until all eight candles are lit on the eighth night. Each night the song of praise, *Ma'Oz Tzur* (Rock of Ages), is sung once the candles are lit.

This **Hannukah celebration** takes place for eight nights in Jewish homes all over the world. Each evening is filled with light and song and gifts for the children.

Once the candles are lit, games are played, including one with a spinning top called a *Sevivon,* or dreidel. In Israel, the top has four letters on it, standing for the words: *Ness Gadol Haya Po* – A Great Miracle Happened Here. Outside of Israel, the last word on the top is: *Sham,* or there.

It is traditional to eat fried foods during Hannukah, because of the symbolism of oil. Favorite Hannukah foods include jelly doughnuts (called *Sufganiot*) and potato pancakes (called *Levivot,* or *Latkes*).

Latkes

Potato Pancakes

About 16

PARVE

Ingredients:

5 large baking potatoes
2 eggs
4 tbs flour
1 tsp baking powder
1 tsp salt
½ tsp white pepper
Oil for frying

Latkes taste best right from the pan. But if you are not serving them right away, these directions will help you get crisp latkes - and they're best when they're crisp!
Some prefer to add onion while others will eat the latkes with sugar or preserves.

Directions:

Grate potatoes. Place in strainer and rinse with cold water. Let drain about 10 minutes, press out water and combine with eggs, flour, baking powder, salt and pepper in large bowl.

Pour oil ¼" deep in a frying pan and heat. When oil is hot, place 1 tbs batter for each latke in pan and flatten with the back of a spoon.

Reduce heat a little and let latkes fry 5 minutes on each side, until golden.

Place finished latkes on paper towels to drain and cool. Layer the cool latkes on foil (no more than 2 layers), wrap in heavy foil and freeze.

To use:

Heat in a 400°C (800°F) oven about 12 minutes. They will taste fresh-baked.

PARVE

Sufganiot à la Margit

Deep-Fried Jelly Doughnuts

Makes 24

Ingredients:

15 g (½ oz) fresh yeast
½ cup lukewarm water
4 tbs melted parve
  margarine
2½-3 cups flour
1 egg yolk
3 tbs sugar
½ tsp salt
½ tsp nutmeg
½ tsp vanilla or cardamom
Grated rind of ½ lemon
4 cups oil for frying (can be
  used again)
Confectioners' sugar
Jam

Jelly doughnuts are traditional Hannukah treats because they are deep-fried in oil, reminding us of the oil used in the ancient Temple. It takes some practice to make crisp, light doughnuts, but everyone will agree that it's worth the effort.

Directions:

Crumble yeast into water with ½ teaspoon sugar. Allow to dissolve for 5 minutes.

Combine flour, sugar, salt, cardamom or vanilla and nutmeg into a bowl. Make a well and pour the dissolved yeast in the middle.

Add the margarine and egg yolk and mix to a soft dough. It should not be dry. Cover and allow to rise for 1½ hours.

Roll out the dough to about 1½ cm (¾") thickness on a heavily floured board or surface.

Cut round doughnuts with the help of a glass or 3" cookie cutter and allow them to rise on a baking sheet covered with a kitchen towel.

Heat the oil in a deep frying pan up to 180°C (375°F), (use a frying thermometer or test the heat with a piece of white bread; if the bread gets brown in the hot oil in 1 minute, then the oil has reached the right frying temperature).

Drop 3-4 doughnuts at a time in the oil and fry, covered, for 2 minutes. Remove the lid and turn them and fry them for 2 minutes, this time uncovered, until they are golden brown.

Remove onto paper towels or a colander so excess oil can drip away.

Sprinkle with confectioner's sugar and inject with jam.

Sufganiot are best served warm.

Chicken in Three Marinades

Serves 4

MEAT

Ingredients:
1 chicken
1 cup dry white wine,
  bouillon or water

Marinade No.1:
¼ cup olive oil
1 tsp salt
Juice of 1 lemon
1 tsp paprika
2 tsp curry powder

Marinade No.2:
¼ cup olive oil
1 tsp salt
Juice of 1 lemon
1 tsp oregano
1 tsp thyme
1 crushed clove of garlic

Marinade No.3:
¼ cup olive oil
1 tsp salt
Juice of 1 lemon
3-4 tbs chopped mixed green
  herbs - parsley, scallions,
  fresh dill, or others

Directions:
Divide the chicken into 4-6 pieces.

Mix ingredients for any one of the marinades.

Brush the chicken pieces with the marinade.

Arrange them in an oven-proof dish.

Pour the wine, bouillon or water around the chicken.

Put the dish in a preheated oven and bake at 220°C (425°F) for 45 minutes.

Serve with baked potatoes and crisp green salad.

MEAT

Shepherd's Pie
Potato Pie with Spicy Stuffing
Serves 4

Ingredients:

400 g (1 lb) veal meat or
  chicken breast
1 large onion
2 tbs oil
1 clove of garlic
1 tsp coriander powder
½ tsp ground ginger
Salt and pepper
1 cup frozen green peas and
  carrots
700 g (1½ lbs) potatoes
1 egg
2-3 tbs matza meal or bread
  crumbs

> *Gathered around the warm
> and cosy candle-lights of
> Hannukah, it is pleasant to
> have some easy and
> delicious dishes which can
> be prepared beforehand –
> Shepherd's Pie, for
> example.*

Directions:

Wash the unpeeled potatoes and boil in salted water
until cooked.

While the potatoes are cooking, cut the meat into
very fine pieces and dice the onion.

Heat oil in a pot and fry the meat and onion, add the
crushed clove of garlic and stir well.

Add the spices and allow the filling to simmer until
meat is tender.

Add the frozen vegetables and continue cooking for
about 5 minutes.

Put the filling into an oven-proof dish.

Peel the boiled potatoes and mash with a fork. Add
the matza meal and egg.

Put the mashed potatoes on top of the filling and
spread evenly to the sides of the dish.

Brush with a little olive oil and put the dish in a
preheated oven for 25 minutes at 220°C (425°F),
until the potato topping is golden brown.

Serve with crispy green salad, or cucumbers cut into
long sticks, and warm French Bread.

Mousaka

Meat and Eggplant Casserole

Serves 8

MEAT

Ingredients:

1 kg (2 lbs) eggplants
Oil for frying

Meat Sauce:

1 large onion
1 clove of garlic
3 tbs oil or parve margarine
1 kg (2 lbs) ground meat
1 tsp salt
½ tsp pepper
1 tsp oregano
1 tsp thyme
2 tbs fresh chopped parsley
1 cup crushed tomatoes
*3-4 fresh tomatoes for
  garnish*

Béchamel Sauce:

2½ tbs parve margarine
½ cup flour
2 cups bouillon
½ tsp white pepper
½ tsp ground nutmeg

---

*This dish can be taken out
of the freezer and warmed
just before serving,
accompanied by a green
salad.*

Directions:

Wash the eggplants, slice them in 1 cm (½") thick slices, sprinkle with kitchen salt and put them aside in a colander for ½ an hour.

Rinse the slices and pat them with a paper towel.

Heat the oil in a pan and fry the eggplant until light brown, remove and drain on thick paper towels (the eggplant absorbs a lot of oil).

Meanwhile, prepare the meat sauce:

Peel and dice the onion and garlic and fry in the hot margarine or oil until just transparent.

Add the meat and stir with a fork.

Add the chopped tomatoes and the spices and stir very well, allow to simmer for 10 minutes.

Béchamel is prepared separately:

Melt the margarine, add the flour and stir well with a wooden spoon.

When the margarine has absorbed all the flour, change to a metal whisk, and pour in the bouillon while stirring. As the sauce gets creamy and small bubbles appear, lower the heat and allow to simmer for 5 minutes. Keep whisking or the sauce will get lumpy. Remove from the heat and add nutmeg and pepper.

Arrange the Mousaka:

Grease an oven-proof dish – about 23x33x5 cm (9"x13"x2") or, if intending to freeze, use an oven-to-freezer dish.

Cover the bottom with a layer of fried eggplant slices, pour the meat sauce over, then again a layer of eggplant.

Finally, pour the béchamel sauce over everything and put the dish in a preheated oven at 180°C (375°F) for 40 minutes. Garnish with slices of fresh tomatoes and chopped parsley.

MEAT

Angriyee
Veal with Fragrant Vegetables
Serves 8-10

Ingredients:

2 kg (4 lb) veal shoulder
2 eggplants
3 large beets
3 large potatoes
2 large tomatoes
1 onion
2 cloves of garlic
1 tsp ground coriander
½ tsp ground ginger
Juice of 1 lemon
2 tbs sugar
Salt and pepper
A few sprigs of mint or
    parsley
Olive oil for frying

Directions:

Roast the veal for a couple of hours, possibly a day before, and allow to cool.

Slice the eggplant and sprinkle with kitchen salt, set aside for ½ hour.

Peel and slice the potatoes and dry them thoroughly.

Heat oil in a pan, fry the potatoes lightly on both sides and drain on a thick paper towel. Set them aside.

Dry the eggplant slices and fry them light brown in the hot oil, drain on thick absorbent paper.

Boil the unpeeled beets until tender and allow to cool – then peel and slice. Wash and cut tomatoes into slices.

Peel and chop the onion and garlic and fry together with coriander and ginger. Add ½ cup of sauce from the veal roast, the lemon juice and the sugar.

Cut the meat into thin slices.

Lightly grease an oven-proof dish with oil and arrange the slices of meat and vegetables in layers.

Top with tomato slices and pour the sauce over.

Sprinkle with chopped mint leaves or parsley and cover.

Bake the dish in a preheated oven at 200°C (400°F) for 30 minutes.

Angriyee: This traditional Indian delicacy may sound "angry", but it's actually a very happy combination of meat and vegetables! When served with bread and salad, this makes a filling meal. Remember when serving, dig down to the bottom in order to get to all the layers.

Moist Pineapple Cake

Serves 8

PARVE

Ingredients:

200 g (8 oz) parve
margarine
1 cup sugar
4 eggs
2½ cups flour
1 tsp baking powder
1 cup ground nuts
1 cup crushed pineapple
(from can)

Garnish:

Semi-sweet chocolate and/or
slices of pineapple.

Directions:

Beat magarine and sugar until smooth and creamy.

Add the eggs, one at a time, and whisk well after each.

Combine flour, nuts and baking powder, and stir into the dough.

Fold in the crushed pineapple.

Pour in a greased baking dish and bake in a preheated oven at 170°C (375°F) for 1 hour.

Garnish cake with melted chocolate and thin slices of pineapple.

Variation:
Spread melted chocolate on cake, sprinkle with shredded coconut and decorate with orange or tangerine slices.

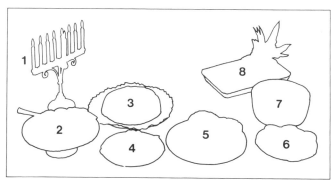

Hannukah, Festival of Lights

PARVE

Orange and Lemon Sorbet
Serves 8

Ingredients:
3½ cups sugar
1 liter (4 cups) water
8 oranges
4 lemons
Chocolate-coated orange
  peels

Directions:
Boil sugar and water together until sugar is melted.

Remove from the heat and allow to cool completely.

Add the juice of 8 oranges, grated rind of 4 oranges and the juice of 4 lemons and stir well.

Then strain the juice and pour into a ring mold or any other desired form and put in the freezer.

In order to prevent the sorbet from getting too hard, take out and stir the juice about 4 times during the first couple of hours until completely frozen.

When serving, unmold and garnish with chocolate-coated orange peels.

Chocolate Nut Cake

Serves 6-8

PARVE

Ingredients:

200 g (8 oz) parve
  margarine
1 cup sugar
200 g (8 oz) pistachio paste*
  or almond paste
4 eggs, separated
1 cup walnuts, chopped
60-70 g (3 oz) dark, parve
  semi-sweet chocolate,
  chopped
1¾ cups flour
1 tsp baking powder
Juice of 1 orange
Grated rind of ½ an orange

Garnish:

Melted chocolate
Green pistachio nuts

* Pistachio Paste:
Check if available at the
Gourmet Counter of your
market. If not available,
substitute 6 oz shelled
pistachios, ground in a
food processor.

Directions:

Beat margarine and sugar until fluffy and pale yellow.

Add pistachio or almond paste and beat again.

Add egg yolks one at a time and whisk well as each is added.

Add the grated rind of ½ an orange.

Combine nuts, chocolate, flour and baking powder and stir in margarine mixture, alternating with the orange juice.

Beat egg whites until stiff and fold into the dough.

Pour into a greased cake dish and bake in a preheated oven at 170°C (370°F) for 1 hour.

When cake is baked and cooled, brush with melted chocolate and sprinkle with pistachio nuts.

DAIRY

Pistachio Ice Cream à la Hannukah
Serves 12

Ingredients:
200 g (8 oz) pistachio paste
4 eggs, separated
½ cup confectioner's sugar
½ liter (2 cups) whipping
  cream
1 cup walnuts
1 tbs brandy or orange
  liqueur

Optional:
½ tsp green food coloring
Pistachio nuts
Almond oil for the mold

Garnish:
Kiwi
Green grapes
Whipped cream

Directions:
Beat egg yolks and sugar until fluffy and pale yellow in color.

Add pistachio paste and liqueur and beat again vigorously. Add food coloring, if desired.

Whip cream until soft peaks form and fold into the mixture.

Beat two egg whites stiff and fold them in carefully.

Coarsely chop the walnuts and add them into the cream.

Brush a ring mold with almond oil, if desired and pour the pistachio ice cream into it.

Freeze for at least 3-4 hours.

Dip mold in hot water to unmold.

Garnish with fruit and/or whipped cream and pistachios.

> *If the mold is greased with a little almond oil, the ice cream will slip out easily.*

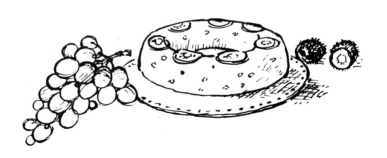

Tova's Brownies

Makes 50-60 pieces

PARVE

Ingredients:
350 g (14 oz) parve
  margarine
3¼ cups sugar
5 tsp vanilla
7 eggs
1¾ cups flour
¾ cup cocoa
1 cup chopped hazelnuts,
  almonds or peanuts

> *A delicious candy-like cake
> for coffee.*

Directions:
Melt the margarine in a large pot.

Remove from heat and add sugar and vanilla, and stir well with a wooden spoon – do not use an electric mixer!

Put eggs in, one at a time, beating between each egg.

Combine the flour, cocoa and nuts and add to the mixture, beating until all ingredients are mixed well.

Pour the batter into a well-greased baking pan about 40 x 30 cm (16" x 12") and bake in a preheated oven at 180°C (350°F) for 40 minutes.

When ready, cut the cake while still hot in small squares and place on cooling rack.

Serve in fluted cupcake cups.

These keep well in a tightly-sealed cookie jar.

PARVE

Pastry Dough
Makes 30 cookies or 2 pie crusts

Ingredients:
2 ½ cups flour
200 g (8 oz) parve
  margarine
½ cup sugar

> *Pastry dough is easy and*
> *tasty.*
> *It can keep in the refrigerator*
> *for 2 weeks or in the freezer*
> *for a year.*
> *We use this pastry dough for*
> *pies, tarts, etc.*
> *I have taught this formula to*
> *the kids in school in order to*
> *memorize an easy recipe,*
> *always at hand (or rather, in*
> *the head) if a sudden need for*
> *something sweet arises and*
> *the cookbook is far away!*

Directions:
Cut the cold margarine into the flour and crumble a little with your fingers until it resembles grated parmesan cheese.

Add sugar and egg and just gather together the dough – do not knead it.

Roll to a long sausage shape, pack in foil and chill for at least ½ an hour.

Pistachio Cookies
Makes approx. 15-20 cookies

Ingredients:
1 portion pastry dough

Filling:
200 g (8 oz) pistachio paste,
  soft marzipan or almond
  paste, if pistachio paste is
  not available

Garnish:
Crystallized sugar, whole
  blanched hazelnuts,
  maraschino cherries, fresh
  berries

Directions:
Roll out dough between 2 baking sheets of paper and cut round cookies with the help of a coffee cup or cookie cutter, about 6-7 cm (3 inches) wide.

In half of the cookies, cut a small circle of about 3 cm (1½ inches) in diameter, to form rings.

Brush the rings with beaten egg and sprinkle crystallized sugar on them.

Arrange all the cookies (the rings and the plain circles) on a baking tray covered with baking paper and bake in preheated oven at 200°C (400°F) for 12 minutes.

Remove to cooling rack and spread pistachio cream on the whole cookies and top with the baked rings to make sandwich cookies.

Garnish the middle with either a blanched hazelnut, maraschino cherry or a fresh berry.

"And Jacob gave Esau bread and lentil porridge and he ate and drank and rose up, and went his way..."

Genesis, Chapter 25, Verse 34

Tevet
Winter and Warm Soups

After Hannukah, winter is in full swing. There are no Jewish holidays in Tevet, but delicious warm soups can help maximize the enjoyment of this month.

Soups play an important role in menu planning because they are so versatile. Soups can be filled with meat, vegetables and grains such as rice or pasta, and can comprise a whole meal in themselves.

Clear soup with a little garnish can be served as a light, first course to a dinner, or a heartier soup can quench the appetite and provide enough nutrition to offer an alternative to a more expensive, multi-course meal.

For these reasons, it's a good idea to keep a variety of soup bases on hand. These bases can be used to create sauces, stews and many kinds of soup. Soup bases should be kept in the freezer until use. Soup bases are rich in flavor and can be diluted for cooking. The soup can be varied with the addition of rice, pasta, vegetables, meat, or croutons. Food stores carry a variety of soups in different forms: frozen or dehydrated (freeze-dried) soup stock, powdered soup mix, canned soup concentrate, etc. Many of these are packaged in individual portions, making it easy to include them in recipes.

You can also prepare a soup base to fit your own taste and pocketbook. Use meat bones, small pieces of meat, or poultry parts (such as the neck), and add vegetables in season to cut costs. You can also use parts of vegetables which you might otherwise discard, such as the leaves of a leek, parsley stems, celery root or leaves, etc.

The variations and combinations are countless. There's nothing better than to come home from work on a cold winter evening to the welcoming smell of a hearty soup on the stove. And a chilly winter weekend can be warmed up instantly with a cup of rich, hot soup. Because the ingredients may vary with each new batch, every soup has a flavor and soul of its own.

Beef Bouillon

Makes 3 liters (3 quarts)

Ingredients:
1 kg (2 lbs) beef and veal
  bones
½ kg (1 lb) meat scraps
3 liters (3 quarts) water
1 tsp salt
1 tsp peppercorns
5 carrots
5 celery sticks
3 bay leaves
1 onion
8 sprigs of parsley

Optional:
2 egg whites and their shells

---

*Consommé is a clear soup.
Egg whites make the soup
clear as the proteins
encircle the loose particles
in the stock and can easily
be strained away.*

Directions:
Put bones and meat in a large pot.

Cover with water, add salt, pepper, carrots, celery and onion.

Bring slowly to a boil, skim as necessary and allow to simmer for about 2½ hours.

Add bay leaves and parsley and allow to simmer for another half an hour.

Strain stock and allow to chill. Remove the fat that rises to the top.

Clear soups, bouillons or consommé are a perfect start to a festival dinner.

Consommé is made by dropping 2 egg whites and 2 shells in the soup. Bring the soup slowly to a boil while stirring.

Reduce heat and allow to simmer for 20 minutes. Strain the stock again through a thin damp cloth.

Serve with meatballs or put a raw egg yolk in each portion.

Chicken Stock

Makes 3 liters (3 quarts)

Ingredients:
2 kg (4 lbs) chicken bones
  (wings, necks, etc.)
3 liters (3 quarts) water
1 tsp salt
½ tsp whole peppercorns
1 large onion
3 carrots
Bouquet of different greens
  (celery, parsley, dill)

Directions:
Prepare as for beef stock, except cooking time is 1½ hours. Skimming as necessary.

Then add the bouquet of greens and allow to simmer for 30 minutes.

Strain, chill and remove fat.

Fish Stock

Makes 2 liters (2 quarts)

PARVE

Ingredients:
2 kg (4 lbs) fish bones or
   inexpensive whole fish
2 onions
2-3 bay leaves
2 carrots
1 tsp peppercorns
2 cloves
1 tsp salt
2 liters (2 quarts) water
Bouquet of fresh parsley,
   thyme and bay leaves.

Directions:
Put all ingredients in a large pot and cover with water.

Bring slowly to a boil and simmer for about 1 hour on low heat.

Skim if necessary.

Strain stock through a fine sieve.

Can be frozen in smaller portions and used as a base for fish soups and sauces.

Vegetable Stock

Makes 2 liters (2 quarts)

PARVE

Ingredients:
5 carrots
4 celery sticks
3 onions
1 parsnip
2 cloves of garlic
3 whole cloves
Bouquet of parsley, thyme,
   and bay leaves
5 fresh tomatoes or 2 cups
   tomato juice
Salt and pepper
1½ liters (6 cups) of water

Directions:
Wash and slice carrots, onions, parsnips and tomatoes and celery sticks.

Put into a large pot; add all the other ingredients, cover with water and bring to a boil.

Allow to simmer, covered for 1 hour.

Strain through a fine sieve.

This soup is a good basis for soups and sauces.

MEAT

Midwinter Meat Stew

Serves 10

Ingredients:

2 tbs parve margarine

1 large onion, sliced

1 clove of garlic

500 g (1 lb) boneless cooked
meat or poultry or small
cooked meatballs

8 cups meat stock
(homemade or made from
soup powder)

3 large potatoes, peeled and
diced

3 carrots, sliced

1 cup celery root, diced

1 cup frozen green peas

1 cup tomatoes, chopped

Salt and pepper

1 tsp basil leaves or powder

1 cup rice, small soup
noodles or macaroni

1 cup chick peas (soaked
overnight and cooked until
tender)

3 tbs chopped parsley

Directions:

Melt margarine in a large pot, brown onion and garlic.

Add the peeled and cut vegetables and stir well.

Sprinkle the basil and pour in the bouillon slowly.

Add the meat, rice or chick peas. Bring slowly to a boil and allow the soup to simmer for 30 minutes.

If you prefer noodles, spaghetti, or macaroni, then add them just 10 minutes before serving.

Serve hot, in deep soup plates and garnish with freshly chopped parsley.

> One can use the leftovers of
> meat or vegetables and add
> seasonal greens.
> Serve the soup with whole
> wheat rolls spread with
> liver paté (see page 58).

Shorba

Chicken Soup with Rice

Serves 4

MEAT

Ingredients:

1 tbs oil
½ chicken
3-4 ripe tomatoes
½ tsp salt
1 tsp pepper
½ tsp turmeric
½ cup rice
1 tsp cardamom
2-3 cups water

Shorba, in Arabic, means soup.
In the Middle East, soup is often a meal in itself – containing vegetables, meat and rice.

Shorba soup is a nutritious meal and is a very popular dish at Middle Eastern tables.

Directions:

Cut the chicken in small portions and brown in a little oil.

Chop the tomatoes and add them to the chicken.

Sprinkle with salt, pepper and turmeric.

Stir well.

Add 1 cup water, bring slowly to a boil and allow to simmer on low heat until chicken is nearly tender.

Add another 1¼ cup water.

Rinse the rice thoroughly and add to the pot.

Bring to a boil and add cardamom.

Allow to simmer for 30 minutes.

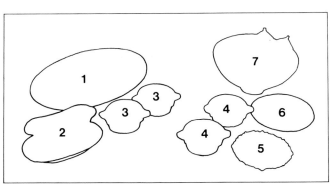

Tevet, Tu B'Shvat

Hamood

Sweet and Sour Soup

Serves 4

Ingredients:

2 tbs oil
1 small onion
½ chicken
½ tsp turmeric
1 tsp pepper
1 tbs tomato purée
2-3 sticks of celery or mint
½ cup raisins
1 tsp salt
1 tbs sugar
Juice of one lemon
1-2 squashes or ½ kg (1 lb)
  pumpkin

Directions:

Sautée the onion lightly in hot oil.

Cut the chicken in small pieces and add to the onion. Add turmeric. Stir well.

Add salt, pepper, tomato purée, celery or mint and raisins.

Dissolve sugar and lemon juice in 2½ cups water and pour into the pot.

Bring to a boil slowly and allow to simmer until the chicken is nearly tender.

Slice the squashes or pumpkin and add to the soup.

Simmer until chicken pieces are completely cooked.

Hamood:
A sweet and sour soup from the Near and Far East. The soup is also used as a sauce for main courses.

Hamood can serve as a main course, if kuba (see page 90-91) is added to it and it is served with boiled white rice.

Chinese Hot and Sour Soup
Serves 4

MEAT

Ingredients:

1 liter (4 cups) chicken broth
2 carrots, cut into
   match-sticks
100 g (4 oz) mushrooms,
   sliced
3 scallions, chopped
$\frac{1}{2}$-1 cup green peas
3 tbs soy sauce
3 tbs herb vinegar
2 tsp sugar
$\frac{1}{4}$ tsp cayenne or chili
1 tsp black pepper
Salt to taste
2 tbs cornflour
4 tbs water
2 eggs

Directions:

Warm the chicken broth and add the sliced vegetables and the peas.

Allow the vegetables to cook a couple of minutes and then add the soy sauce, vinegar, sugar, cayenne pepper, and salt, if necessary.

Pour the cornflour into the boiling soup.

Beat for 2-3 minutes until the soup thickens.

Whip the eggs in a small bowl with a fork and pour in a thin stream into the boiling soup, then turn off the heat.

Serve the soup piping hot in small soup bowls.

One of the delightful discoveries of Jewish gastronomy is kosher Chinese food, and there are kosher Chinese restaurants cropping up in many countries.

Kuba (Kibbeh)

Meatballs in Dough

On special occasions – for holidays and Shabbat meals – my mother takes extra time to prepare meatballs that are wrapped in dough and cooked in different dishes or sauces.

These "hidden" meat balls are called Kuba or Kibbeh and are well known in Middle Eastern cuisine, although they differ slightly from country to country in taste. The technique is the same and preparing the dish calls for talent and practice! In fact, they say that some are blessed with especially good hands for creating these delicious meatballs! I have tasted Kuba by many a clever and "blessed" hand and have always enjoyed them.

My friend from Iraq makes the dough with bulgur wheat (parboiled crushed wheat) and the filling with ground mutton or veal. She then forms them into oblong shapes, boils them and then fries them. My mother chooses to make the dough with rice flour and mutton. The filling is also mutton, although more spicy than the first. They are then shaped into small balls and cooked in different sauces and stews, from the spiciest hot to the sour and sweet.

An easier version, which I suggest here is Kuba made with a farina dough. One can make big portions and freeze them, since they can be put directly into boiling sauce. They should simmer 20 minutes.

In this book, Kuba may be used in the following recipes:

page 25: Lal Kuba (instead of just meatballs as mentioned in the recipe)

page 60: Batana Kuba (spicy green pea sauce)

page 88: Hamood (sweet and sour – a child's favorite)

page 141: Bamia Kuba (sweet and sour okra)

Kuba can also be put in any soup which then gets an extra "zing".

Kuba

Makes 30-35

Ingredients:

Dough:
2 ½ cups (1 lb) semolina
   flour
1 egg
1 tsp salt
2 tbs oil
1 cup water

Filling:
500 g (1 lb) ground veal (or
   other meat)
1-2 onions (grated)
1 pinch of salt
Pepper
4 sprigs of mint
6-7 sprigs fresh coriander
½ tsp turmeric
1 tender inner stalk of celery

Directions:

Grate the onions on the coarse side of a grater. Press and discard liquid.

Add the meat, salt, chopped celery or mint and coriander and turmeric.

Combine semolina, egg and oil.

Pour in water gradually, until the dough becomes elastic.

Wet fingers and divide dough into small balls of about 3 cm (1½ inches) in diameter. Flatten each ball in your palm to about 6 cm (3 inches) in diameter.

Place a teaspoon of the filling in the middle of the dough and carefully close the dough around the filling, without damaging the dough.

Roll between the palms of your hands and form a complete round ball.

Place kuba on a wet plate.

They can now either be frozen for later use or dropped into boiling sauces or soups.

Kuba need about 20 minutes of cooking with the pot cover slightly open.

The dough absorbs the taste of the soup or sauce that it is cooked in, and that is what makes the Kuba so deliciously special.

> *"...When you enter the country, and you plant a fruit tree..."*
> *Leviticus, Chapter 19, Verse 23*

Tu B'Shvat

"Tu B'Shvat" , the 15th day of Shvat, falls in February, and is the Jewish Arbor Day.

Tu B'Shvat is also called "The New Year for Trees", and is considered a half holiday. It falls near the end of the Israeli winter, when the seasonal cold and rain begin to let up. At this time, thoughts turn to Spring and new growth.

New life comes in the form of bright green leaves, following the winter hibernation. Shvat is the month when the almond trees bloom with beautiful white and pink blossoms, and the citrus groves are filled with the aroma of orange blossoms. In Israel, Tu B'Shvat is a day when adults and children visit groves and forests to plant trees.

Fruit – both fresh and dried – is eaten to symbolize the new growth, and songs are sung about Spring, trees and flowers, and nature in general.

Many Jews live in countries where the ground is frozen solid during February – thus eliminating the possibility of planting trees. In these countries it is traditional for the Jewish community to collect money to be used to plant trees in Israel. Luckily, the other part of Tu B'Shvat's traditional celebration, singing songs of Spring, and eating fruit, is something which can be done anywhere in the world – no matter what the season! In some schools, each of the pupils brings in some fruit, and a large bowl of fruit salad is made for everyone to enjoy.

Meatballs in Gala

(in Cranberry Sauce)

Serves 4

MEAT

Ingredients:

4 tbs parve margarine for frying
500 g (1 lb) ground meat
1 egg
1 slice of stale bread or ½ a matza soaked in water
1 tsp bouillon powder (meat or vegetable)
½ tsp ground cloves
1 tsp pepper
1 tsp ground ginger
125 g (5 oz) small mushrooms
1 cup blanched almonds
¾ cup small frozen onions
1 cup baby carrots
300 g (12 oz) small round potatoes

Optional:

1 can artichoke hearts

Sauce:

340 g (¾ lb) fresh cranberries
½ cup raisins
1 tsp ground ginger
½ tsp ground cloves
1 pinch cayenne
½ tsp cinnamon
¼ cup sugar
1 cup water
1 cup dry kosher red wine

Directions:

Mix the ground meat with the egg, soaked bread (press out the water first), bouillon powder, cloves, ginger and pepper.

Form small meatballs about 3cm (1½ inch) in diameter and fry them in half the amount of margarine.

Remove them to a colander or absorbant paper, to drain excess fat. Wash the mushrooms in running water and cut off the root. Fry them for a couple of minutes and remove to absorbant paper.

Fry the blanched almonds, small onions, baby carrots and, if used, artichokes too; fry each ingredient separately and then remove to absorbant paper.

Boil the unpeeled potatoes for 10 minutes, then peel them.

Melt the remaining margarine and sautée the potatoes until brown. Drain off excess fat.

Arrange the different fried ingredients in an oven-proof dish and cover.

Sauce:

Combine all ingredients for the sauce (except the wine) in a pot and allow to simmer for 10 minutes.

Add red wine and bring to boil, allow to simmer for 2 minutes.

To serve: pour the sauce over the meatballs and vegetables. Put the dish (covered) in a warm oven at 170°C (340°F) for 15 min.

Can be served with rice.

DAIRY

Cream Cheese Crescents with Dried Fruit
Makes 40

Ingredients:
Pastry:
300 g (12 oz) butter
3 cups flour
½ tsp salt
150 g (6 oz) cream cheese

Filling:
¾ cup dried apricots
1 cup dried dates
¾ cup yellow raisins
½ tsp cardamom
1 cup chopped nuts

Optional:
1 tsp rosewater

> **This filling also tastes delicious as a spread on bread or biscuits!**

Directions:
Cut the butter into the flour with a knife until it reaches a "gritty" texture.

Add the salt and cheese and roll into a ball.

Allow to chill for 1 hour before use.

Meanwhile, make the filling:

Mix apricots, dates and raisins in a pot. Pour 1 cup water in and allow to cook for 5 minutes.

Cool the fruit and then grind in a chopper or grinder.

Add cardamom and chopped nuts and, if desired, rosewater.

Roll the chilled dough between 2 layers of waxed paper.

When rolled, the dough should be 3mm (¹/₁₆ th inch) thick.

Cut round cookies with a cookie cutter or a glass – about 5-6 cm (3 inches) in diameter.

Put a teaspoonful of the filling on each piece and fold over, to form a crescent shape.

Seal the sides by pressing closed with a fork.

Put the pastry crescents onto a baking tray covered with waxed paper.

Brush with beaten egg.

Bake in a preheated oven at 200°C (400°F) for 20 minutes.

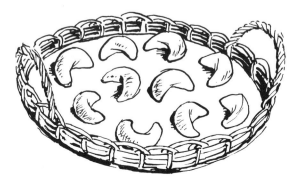

Armenian Pastries

Makes 30-40 pieces

PARVE

Ingredients:
2½ cups flour
200 g (8 oz) parve
  margarine
½ cup sugar
1 egg
1 tsp vanilla

Filling:
1½ cups dried dates
¾ cup yellow raisins
1 cup chopped nuts
1 tsp cardamom

Optional:
1 tsp rosewater

Garnish:
Egg
Sliced almonds
Pistachio or hazelnuts

---

*In this recipe, I was
inspired by the fragrant
spices of my Armenian
neighbor.
Variation:
For the filling, other dried
fruits can also be used,
such as figs or fig paste and
chopped nuts.*

Directions:
Cut the cold margarine into the flour.

Add sugar, egg and vanilla.

Combine the ingredients with a light hand – do not knead as the dough will get too soft.

Chill the dough for ½ an hour.

Meanwhile make the filling:

Combine dates and raisins with 1 cup of water and boil for 5-6 minutes.

Remove from heat, cool and then grind in a chopper or grinder. Then add the chopped nuts, cardamom and rosewater.

Roll the cold pastry dough between 2 layers of waxed paper to avoid sticking to the board.

Cut long strips of about 10 x 20 cm (4" x 8").

Arrange the filling in the middle of the strip and fold the sides up towards the middle, so they overlap one another.

Brush top with beaten egg and sprinkle with nuts.

Cut cakes in diagonal slices and put them on a baking tray covered with waxed paper.

Bake pastries in a preheated oven at 200°C (400°F) for 12-15 minutes.

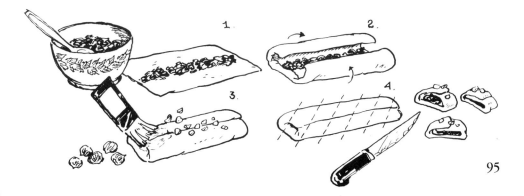

PARVE

Apple Blackberry Tart

Serves 6-8

Ingredients:

Dough:

2½ cups flour

200 g (8 oz) parve margarine

½ cup confectioner's sugar

1 egg

1 tsp vanilla

Filling:

500 g (1 lb) thick applesauce

3 bananas

4 tbs blackberry jam

Grated rind and juice of half a lemon

Garnish:

Blanched and chopped almonds and/or crystallized sugar

Dairy variation: serve with whipped or sour cream.

Directions:

Combine all ingredients for dough with a light hand, form into a ball and chill for at least 30 min.

Divide the dough into three pieces.

Prepare applesauce (see Apple Pie, p. 56) or buy ready-made.

Add grated lemon rind.

Peel and thinly slice bananas, and pour lemon juice over them.

Line the bottom of a cake dish (with removable sides) with ⅓ of the dough, bake for 10 min. at 200°C (400°F). Allow to cool.

Line the sides of the cake dish with the next ⅓ of the dough.

Spread jam on the bottom, then arrange half the amount of banana slices over it, then ½ of the applesauce, then another layer of banana slices and cover with applesauce.

Roll out the remaining ⅓ of dough to fit like a lid over the cake, and cut a few holes for moisture to escape while baking.

Brush top with beaten egg and sprinkle with chopped nuts and/or sugar.

Bake in preheated oven at 200°C (400°F) for 40 min.

"...and the month was turned to them from sorrow to joy, and from mourning to holiday: that they should make them days of feasting and joy..."
From the "Book of Esther"

Purim

Purim is celebrated on the 14th day of Adar, which usually falls in late February or early March. Purim celebrates an event which took place in ancient Persia (possibly around the date 480 B.C.E.). The story is told in an ancient scroll, the **Book of Esther**, which is read aloud each year on Purim.

The story of Purim: Haman, an evil advisor to the Persian king, Ahasuerus, had convinced the king to have the Jews destroyed. Lots were chosen to pick the day for the massacre and the king issued a decree that all Jews were to be put to death on the 14th day of Adar. (The word Purim means lots.)

Before the massacre could be carried out, **Queen Esther** intervened. Esther was the favorite wife of Ahasuerus and, unbeknownst to him, a Jewess. Esther's uncle, Mordechai, was an official in Ahasuerus' court. Esther conducted a campaign in an effort to convince the king to halt the massacre. For 3 days Esther fasted and prayed, and finally convinced Ahasuerus of the wickedness of Haman's plan. The **Fast of Esther** is observed every year on the 13th of Adar, followed by the joyous celebration of Purim on Adar 14th. In walled cities, such as Jerusalem, it is traditional to celebrate Purim on the next day, the 15th of Adar.

This tradition dates back to the days of ancient Persia. In the walled city of Shushan, the Purim festival was held one day late, presumably because the news of the Jews' redemption did not reach the people there until the next day.

The **Purim celebration** is one of joy and merriment. It is a kind of Jewish carnival: The children dress up in costumes and the story of Esther is told in words and song in synagogues and meeting places. Whenever Haman's name is mentioned, noisemakers are used to drown out the evil word. It is traditional to drink wine, and on this day, drinking to excess is even condoned! Baskets of fruit, pastry and sweets are prepared and decorated colorfully. These are delivered to friends, neighbors and relatives and especially to the elderly and the poor, so that no one is left out of the joyous celebration.

The most **traditional Purim food** is the triangular pastry called *Hamantaschen* – Haman's Pockets, in Europe. In Israel, the pastries are called *"Oznei Haman"* – Haman's Ears! This pastry is most commonly filled with poppy seeds. Some say the tradition of triangular-shaped pastry comes from the three-cornered hat thought to have been worn by Haman. In India, we often ate Sambusak, a triangular pastry made with chick peas or potato filling (see following pages).

MEAT

Mahasha

Stuffed Vegetables

Serves 4-6

Ingredients:

4 large onions
4 large tomatoes
4 leaves of Chinese lettuce,
  bok choy (optional)
8 blanched grape leaves
  (optional)

Stuffing:

1 cup rice (long grain,
  cooked 5 min.)
200 g (½ lb) ground meat
½ tsp pepper
1 tsp ground ginger
2 cloves of garlic, finely
  chopped
½ tsp allspice
Fresh mint leaves or 1 tsp
  dried mint
1 tsp cardamom
½ tsp ground cloves
½ tsp turmeric
Juice of ½ lemon
1 tbs oil or chicken fat
½ tsp cinnamon

Sauce:

½ cup water
Juice of 2 lemons
1½ tbs sugar
1 pinch of salt
¼ tsp ground cloves
½ tsp cardamom

Directions:

Prepare the vegetables as follows:

Onion: Cut off the root. Peel off the outermost layers, then make a deep cut towards the middle vertically through all layers.

Cover the onions with water and bring to a boil, allowing them to cook for 10-15 minutes. Remove from heat and cool.

Now remove each layer of the onion (as if undressing it) carefully. Chop the few innermost layers and add to the filling later.

Tomatoes: Cut the top of the tomatoes and put aside, as they will be needed as lids when tomatoes are stuffed.

Remove pulp of tomatoes with a spoon, keeping the shell intact. Chop the pulp and add to filling later.

Combine all ingredients for filling, including the pulp of the tomatoes and chopped onion. Mix well.

Fill tomatoes ¾ up and cover each with its own "lid". Arrange in a lightly greased oven-proof dish.

Open the onion layers and put a little filling inside. Roll to close (like a cigar) and arrange near the tomatoes in the dish.

If Chinese lettuce leaves are used, they should be blanched first in boiling water for a minute. Cut the thick white stem and put a little filling on the leaf and roll like spring rolls.

Grape leaves are prepared as the Chinese lettuce.

When all vegetables are stuffed, and arranged in dish, pour sauce over. Cover and bake the mahasha in a preheated oven: first for 15 min. on 250°C (475°F), then for 35 min. on 170°C (350°F).

Turkey Shish Kebab

Serves 6

Ingredients:
1 kg (2 lb) Turkey breast

Optional:
*Small tomatoes and small
  onions*

Marinade:
*¼ cup olive oil
Juice of 2 lemons
Salt and pepper to taste
1 clove of garlic, crushed
1 tbs oregano*

> **Shish Kebab: A Middle
> Eastern specialty, usually
> made of marinated meat,
> mutton or poultry on a
> grill.**

Directions:
Dice the turkey breast in pieces of 3 x 3 cm (1½" x 1½"), soak in marinade and allow to chill for 2 hours.

Put the pieces of turkey on a skewer and grill for 10-15 minutes.

Turn them a couple of times.

Put small tomatoes and onions on other skewers and grill them separately. (Small meat balls can also be used.)

Arrange the skewers on a plate of warm rice pilaf. An easier method would be to sautée the meat pieces in olive oil and then arrange alternately with the tomatoes and onions on the skewers - a decorative dinner!

Shish Kebab Sauce

Serves 6

Ingredients:
*3 tbs olive oil
2 onions
2 cloves of garlic, crushed
1 tsp oregano
1 small can tomato purée
½ -1 cup bouillon or water
Salt and pepper to taste*

Optional:
*Pitted olives
5-6 sprigs of fresh parsley*

Directions:
Peel and cut onions into rings.

Sauté them in hot olive oil until light brown.

Add the crushed garlic while stirring.

Add spices and then tomato purée and water or bouillon and allow to simmer for 5-10 minutes.

Cut the olives into small rings and add them together with the chopped parsley. Serve on the side of the Shish Kebab.

Shish Kebab and sauce is excellent with a good tomato salad.

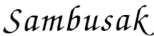

Sambusak

Spicy Turnovers

Makes 25-30

PARVE

Ingredients:

Filling:
2 cups chick peas, soaked
   overnight
750 g (1½ lb) onion
100 g (4 oz) parve
   margarine
Salt and pepper
½ tsp turmeric
1 tsp ground cumin
½-1 cup chopped parsley
2½ cups oil for deep frying
1 tsp cayenne pepper

Dough:
4 cups flour
4 tbs margarine
1½ tbs vinegar
1 tsp salt
1 cup water

> **Sambusak:**
> **Small delicious crescents**
> **filled with spicy ground**
> **chick peas. Good as snacks**
> **or as part of a buffet with**
> **salads and chutney.**
> **Can be frozen before or**
> **after frying.**

Directions:

Begin by preparing the filling:

Cover the soaked chick peas with water and cook in a large pot until soft.

Strain and chop in a chopper or mincer.

Peel and finely slice the onions.

Heat the margarine and sauté the onion in it until light brown.

Add the ground chick peas and fry them with the onions over a low heat for 5-6 minutes.

Add turmeric, cayenne, salt, pepper and cumin.

Sprinkle the chopped parsley and stir well.

Remove from heat and allow to cool.

Meanwhile make the dough:

Melt margarine and combine with remaining ingredients for dough.

Knead to a smooth dough and divide into small balls (the size of a ping-pong ball).

Roll out each ball flat into a circle of about 6-7 cm (2-3 inches) diameter and put a tablespoon of filling on one half and fold the other half over, making a crescent. Seal by pressing closed.

Deep fry until golden brown in hot oil or in a pan with a mixture of oil and margarine.

Serve warm.

Schnitzel Marseillaise
Serves 4

MEAT

Ingredients:
4 veal or turkey schnitzels
1 lemon
Salt and pepper
½ cup bread crumbs
1 egg

Sauce:
2 tbs olive oil
2 onions
3 bell peppers - red, green
  and yellow
2 tomatoes, sliced
½ cup pitted olives
1 sprig of parsley
½ cup white wine or
  bouillon
1 tsp oregano or thyme

Garnish:
½ cup tehina
3 tbs lemon juice
1 egg yolk
Salt

Alternative:
Chopped, skinned tomatoes
Juice of 1 lemon
Salt and pepper
¼ tsp cayenne pepper

Directions:
Marinate meat with lemon juice, salt and pepper.

Allow to chill for about 1 hour.

Then dry meat pieces and coat with egg and bread crumbs.

Fry in margarine for 7-8 minutes on each side. Set aside until sauce is ready.

Heat olive oil in a pan. Peel and slice onion in rings and fry until transparent in oil.

Cut bell peppers in long thin slices. Fry them with the onions. Then, add tomatoes and olives.

Stir very well. Add salt and pepper if desired.

Chop parsley and add it with the oregano and thyme.

Pour the sauce in an oven-proof dish and arrange the schnitzels on top.

Pour the white wine or bouillon over the schnitzels.

Dilute the tehina with lemon juice and 2 tbs water.

Add beaten egg yolks and pour over schnitzels.

Put the dish in preheated oven at 200°C (400°F) for 10 minutes until golden in color.

If tomato alternative is preferred, use instead of tehina sauce garnish.

PARVE

Queen Esther's Cake

Serves 8-10

Ingredients:
Dough:
2½ cups flour
200 g (8 oz) cold parve
   margarine
½ cup sugar
1 egg

Filling:
3 tbs raisins
½ cup orange juice
½ cup sugar
⅔ cup ground poppyseeds
100 g (4 oz) parve
   margarine
3 eggs
1 tbs orange liqueur or
   cognac
1 cup chopped walnuts
½ cup flour

Garnish:
Egg
2 fresh fruits

Directions:
Dough:
Chop cold margarine into flour. Mix with sugar and egg. Allow to chill for about ½ hour.

Filling:
Soak raisins in orange juice for a couple of hours.

Beat margarine, poppyseeds and sugar together until light and fluffy.

Beat in egg yolks, one at a time.

Combine flour, chopped walnuts and add in alternately with orange juice.

Whip egg whites stiff and fold in.

Line bottom and sides of a cake tin with ¾ of the dough. Put in the filling. Roll the remaining dough into strips and lattice over the cake.

Brush with beaten egg.

Bake at 170°C (350°F) for 40 minutes.

Turn off the heat. Allow cake to cool in the oven.

Garnish with peeled and sliced fresh fruit.

Cantaloupe Royale

Serves 4

PARVE

Ingredients:
2 ripe cantaloupe melons
2 tbs Grand Marnier
250 g (½ lb) fresh
   strawberries

Directions:
Cut cantaloupe in halves.

Remove seeds with a spoon.

Put 1 tsp of Grand Marnier in the middle of each half and fill with freshly washed, hulled strawberries.

Serve ½ a melon to each person.

PARVE

Cookies with chocolate coating:

Roll a portion of cookie dough (on page 80) into strips 10 cm (4") long.

Bake for 10 min. at 200°C (400°F). Allow to Cool.

Dip in melted parve chocolate. Allow to dry.

Serve with melons and strawberries.

Desert Delicacy

Directions:
Round off a good menu with something sweet and nutritious like fresh dates.

Remove seeds. Put into each one a blanched and peeled almond or a thin slice of fresh coconut.

Enjoy a bottle of good Israeli wine, together with a festive dinner for Purim. For with wine shall Purim be celebrated "until you cannot see the difference between the cursed Haman and the blessed Mordechai!" (A Talmudic saying)

Hamantashen

"Haman's Ears"

Makes 16 pieces

PARVE

Ingredients:

3 cups flour
150 g (6 oz) parve
   margarine, chilled
2 tbs sugar
1 tsp vanilla or cardemom
2 eggs (1 for glazing)
50 g (2 oz) yeast
½ cup lukewarm water

Filling:

½ cup ground poppyseeds
2 tbs raisins
1 apple, grated
2 tbs jam

**Edible children's masks:
With the same dough, bake
funny masks and write
names with icing and place
on table.**

Directions:

Chop the margarine into flour.

Add one egg, sugar and vanilla or cardemom.

Dissolve yeast in water and add in the above.

Knead into a smooth dough.

Divide dough into 16 small balls (the size of a ping-pong ball).

Roll each ball flat to a circle of 10 cm (4") in diameter.

Mix together all ingredients for the filling.

Put 1 tbs of the filling in the middle, gather the sides up and press together to make a triangle. (See sketch below.)

Put cakes on a baking tray lined with baking paper.

Cover with a kitchen towel and allow to rise for 20 minutes.

Brush with beaten egg and bake at 220°C (400°F) for 15 minutes.

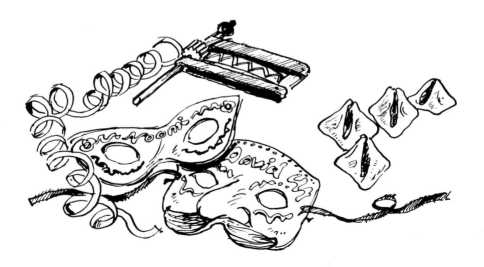

Chocolate Cheesecake

6-8 portions

PARVE

Ingredients:

Dough:
1½ cups flour
4 tbs margarine
¼ cup sugar
1 egg

Filling:
3 eggs
½ cup sugar
100 g (4 oz) semi-sweet
　chocolate
2½ tbs margarine
1 tsp vanilla
1 tbs brandy
Grated rind and juice of ½
　orange
500 g (1 lb) cream cheese
½ cup cake flour
1 tsp instant coffee
　(optional)

Directions:

Dough:
Cut the margarine into the flour and crumble it a little with your fingers until it resembles grated Parmesan cheese.

Add sugar and egg and gather together the dough – do not knead it.

Make a ball and keep in the refrigerator to chill for at least ½ hour.

Filling:
Separate eggs.

Beat yolks and sugar until light and fluffy.

Melt chocolate and margarine. Cool slightly, then add to egg yolks and sugar and mix well.

Add vanilla, brandy, juice and rind of orange and mix well.

Combine cheese and flour and add to mixture.

Beat egg whites until stiff. Fold in.

Press dough on the bottom of a springform pan and pour chocolate-cheese mixture over it.

Sprinkle instant coffee over the top.

Bake in warm oven 180°C (350°F) for 45 min.

Turn the heat off and leave in oven until cool.

Purim

> *"...Let my people go so that they may hold a feast to me in the wilderness."*
> *Exodus, Chapter 5, Verse 1*

> *"Three times a year shall all your men appear before the Lord your God in the place which He shall choose; on the Feast of Unleavened Bread, and the Feast of Weeks, and on the Feast of Booths... Every man shall give as he is able..."*
> *Deuteronomy, Chapter 16, Verses 16,17*

Pesach

Pesach, or Passover, falls in early Spring – on the 15th day of Nissan (usually in late March or early April). Passover is a week-long holiday which celebrates the exodus of the ancient Israelites from their slavery in the land of Egypt.The Passover story tells of the miracles wrought for the Jewish People as Moses led them out of Egypt toward Israel - the Promised Land.

Just as a beloved child has many nicknames, so the holiday of Passover has many names:

Hag Zman Heruteinu – The Festival of Freedom

Hag Ha'Aviv – The Festival of Spring

Hag HaMatzot – The Festival of Unleavened Bread

The most common name for the holiday is Pesach – which means Passover. The name comes from the Biblical story of how an angel passed over the homes of the Israelites and spared them while carrying out a plague which killed the first-born sons of each Egyptian family.

This Pesach story is told each year at a feast called the **Seder**, held on each of the first two nights of the holiday (one night in Israel). The word Seder means order, and refers to the special order of events on that night. The reading of the **Hagaddah** (the Passover story) is accompanied by rituals and traditions which have been carried out in the same way in Jewish homes throughout the world for many generations.

Pesach is different from other holidays because it requires much more preparation: The house must be thoroughly cleaned of every crumb of leavened bread, since bread, pastry and yeast products are forbidden during Pesach. This is in remembrance of the Israelites' hasty flight from Egypt, when there was no time to let the bread rise before baking. Only unleavened bread, called *Matzah*, is eaten during Pesach.

"How does this night differ from all other nights?"
From the Hagaddah read on the Seder nights

This housecleaning ceremony has become a traditional Spring cleaning, when the entire household is made ready for Pesach. In kosher homes, special dishes and utensils are used during Pesach – to avoid contact with any *chametz*, or yeast products.

The entire home takes on a special atmosphere.

The festive **Seder meals** held on the first two nights of Pesach start with a blessing and include prayers of thanksgiving for the Jewish people's redemption from slavery. Three pieces of matzah are covered and put on the table. A special Seder plate is arranged in the center of the table, containing these symbolic foods:

•*Zeroa* – a roasted bone, symbolizing the paschal lamb sacrificed in the Temple in ancient Israel

•*Beitza* – a roasted egg, which symbolizes life

•*Maror* – bitter herbs (horseradish) symbolizing the bitterness of our slavery

•*Karpas* – greens (such as parsely or celery), symbolizing Spring. The greens and egg are dipped in salt water to symbolize the tears of our ancestors

•*Charoset* – a mixture of chopped fruit and wine (see pg. 110) which symbolizes the mortar which our ancestors made for the bricks during their hard labor.

The person leading the seder sits comfortably on a cushioned chair and recites the blessing over the wine. He then takes half of the middle matza and puts it aside for the *afikoman*, the Greek word for desert.

There are different amusing traditions about "playing hide and seek" with the afikoman, to keep the children awake with expectations during the evening. A prize is awarded to the children who find the afikoman at the end of the dinner.

Matzas are also called "Bread of Affliction" to remind us of the bread our forefathers ate on the journey out of Egypt.

During the Seder evening **four glasses of wine** or grape juice are drunk, each symbolizing the terms mentioned in Exodus, Chapter 6, Verses 6-7, when God speaks to the Jewish People:

"...I will bring you out from under the burdens of Egypt"

"...I will deliver you out of their bondage"

"...I will redeem you with an out-stretched arm"

"...I will take you to me for a people."

Even though at first sight, one could feel quite limited in planning menus for Pesach, there are actually many possibilities, and the limitations challenge one's creativity.

The local traditions influence which raw material can be used, like in the case of rice. The local rabbis decide which products are Kosher for Pesach in different countries.

At the end of the holiday, the special dishes and cutlery are set aside for the next year – and we are happy that we had the possibility of celebrating our Exodus from Egypt once more.

For more details on Pesach, one should look into the English Haggadah and commentary books on the subject.

Sephardi Charoset

Oriental Date Paste

Serves 8

PARVE

Ingredients:

500 g (1 lb) fresh dates
½ cup chopped walnuts,
   almonds and/or hazelnuts.
½ cup sweet wine
½ tsp cinnamon or vanilla

Directions:

Wash the dates and remove seeds.

Chop in a grinder or chopper.

Put the dates in a pot and just barely cover with water.

Bring slowly to a boil. Allow to simmer for 40 minutes, while stirring occasionally to avoid sticking to the pot, until the dates have a jam-like consistency.

Remove from heat and add in remaining ingredients.

A delicacy resembling a dark velvety syrup – and it tastes like honey.
As kids in Bombay, we loved to dip in it with wet matzas and "slurp" them down, during the week of Pesach and even afterwards.
It was usually prepared by the family's eldest members who took upon themselves the task of pressing the dates with their fingers for hours, with patience and devotion, as we did not have a grinder.
Preparation for Pesach was extremely demanding. Huge quantities of food were prepared in primitive kitchens, with charcoal stoves and no refrigerating facilities.

MEAT

Knaidalach

Matza Balls

Makes 50

Ingredients:

2 egg yolks
2 tbs melted chicken fat
¾ cup warm bouillon broth
1 cup matza meal
½ tsp salt
½ tsp pepper
1 tbs grated onion
1 tbs chopped parsley
2 egg whites

MEAT

Alternative:
100 g (4 oz) ground meat
can be added to the dough.

Directions:

Beat egg yolks and fat until light and fluffy.

Pour the warm stock in while beating.

Combine the matza meal, salt, pepper, onion and parsley. Then, add to the above ingredients.

Beat the egg whites until stiff and fold in.

Chill the dough for at least 2 hours.

Boil the broth or water in a large pot. Add salt to taste.

With moist hands form the dough into small balls the size of a walnut (they expand a lot while cooking).

You can boil them directly in the soup you will serve them in, or you can make them like this first and reheat them in soup later.

When the soup or water boils, put the matza balls in a few at a time.

When all the balls are in the pot, reduce heat to simmer.

Cover the pot when the matza balls come to the surface.

Fish Cakes

Makes 20 pieces

PARVE

Ingredients:
1 kg (2 lbs) fillets of fish (cod,
  herring, plaice, whitefish or
  carp)
3 large onions
3 tbs chopped dill
1 tsp ground white pepper
1 tsp salt
¼ cup water
½ cup matza meal
3 eggs

**Fish broth for cooking fish
cakes:**
Bones from 2-3 fish
2 onions
3 carrots
2 tsp salt
6 peppercorns
3 bay leaves
Approx. 3 liters (3 quarts)
  water

Directions:
Grind the raw fish fillets twice through the mincer.

Peel and chop the onions very fine and squeeze out
the liquid.

Add onion, salt, pepper, dill, water, matza meal and
egg to the fish.

Allow to chill for about 10 minutes.

Put all the ingredients for fish broth in a large pot.

Bring fish broth to a boil, form fish cake with moist
hands and put them in the boiling broth one at a
time.

When all the fish cakes are in the pot, reduce heat
and simmer on low heat for 1 hour – partially cover
the pot.

Allow the fish to cool down in the broth.

Serve cooked fish cakes cold on a bed of lettuce with
slices of cooked carrots and perhaps some chrain
(see below).

Alternative:
The fish cakes can also be coated with egg and matza meal and fried instead of boiled.
Serve warm with lemon slices and tomato quarters.

Chrain

Horseradish with Beets

PARVE

Ingredients:
400 g (1 lb) horseradish
200 g (½ lb) beets
1 tsp salt
1 tbs sugar
½ cup vinegar

Directions:
Peel and grate horseradish and beets on the fine side
of the grater.

Combine all ingredients and keep in glass jar with a
tight lid.

Keep in cold place.

Chicken with Matza Stuffing

Serves 6-8

Ingredients:

2-2½ kg (4-5 lbs) broiler chicken, boned

Stuffing:

2 matzas
¾ cup bouillon (can be made with chicken soup powder)
500 g (1 lb) ground meat
2 eggs
1 tsp pepper
1 tsp ground ginger
½ tsp ground cloves
1 tsp salt
1 cup chopped fresh pepper (green, yellow, or red)
2 tbs parve margarine

Directions:

It is possible to buy ready-boned poultry at the butcher's, if ordered in advance.

Prepare stuffing by soaking matzas in bouillon. Mix all the remaining ingredients together and stuff in the boned poultry.

Sew together with cotton thread – remember to use one long piece of thread as it will be easier to remove with one pull!

Brush the chicken with melted margarine. Sprinkle with salt and pepper. Bake in oven at 200°C (400°F) for 1½ hours.

Turn off the heat and allow to cool in oven for another 15-20 minutes.

Remove from oven. Remove thread, pulling carefully to get the whole thread out.

Stuffed chicken can be served warm or cold with baked potatoes and cucumber salad.

Meat Loaf with Pepper and Thyme
Serves 6

Ingredients:

1 kg (2 lbs) ground meat
3 eggs
1 tbs bouillon powder
1 tsp pepper
½ cup matza meal
1 tsp thyme
½ cup water
1 chopped onion
Parve margarine or oil to
  grease the dish

Directions:

Combine all ingredients together and mix well.

Form the ground meat into a loaf shape and put in a greased oven-proof dish.

Brush meat with a little oil or melted margarine.

Put in the oven and bake at 200°C (400°F) for 50 minutes.

Serve warm or cold with potato salad and green salad.

MEAT

Tri-Color Chicken Salad

Serves 6-8

Ingredients:

1 kg (2 lbs) broiler chicken
500 g (1 lb) small potatoes
3-4 large tomatoes
1 medium cucumber
3 fresh peppers (red, yellow, and green)
3 avocados
2 lemons
½ iceberg lettuce

Marinade:

½ cup oil
½ cup white wine or lemon juice
1 tsp white pepper
1 tsp salt
1 clove of garlic, crushed
3-4 tbs chopped parsley

Chicken salad is an easy, light and decorative dish for holidays, especially when the holiday starts late in the evening, and heavy meals are not advisable.

Directions:

Boil the chicken in water and a little salt, until tender.

It will be easiest to bone the chicken when still lukewarm. Keep the broth for cooking matza balls (see page 112).

Boil the potatoes, peel and slice.

Slice the tomatoes and cucumber. Cut the peppers in thin rings. Cut the avocados in halves and remove seed. Slice the avocados and sprinkle with a little lemon juice.

Finely slice one lemon and squeeze the juice of the other, and reserve.

Wash and shred the iceberg lettuce.

Arrange on a big serving dish: First a layer of shredded lettuce. Next, add a layer of sliced potatoes and pieces of chicken.

Sprinke with salt and pepper.

Arrange the remaining vegetables in layers respectively.

Garnish with lemon slices.

Beat marinade ingredients together and pour over chicken salad.

Piquant Cucumber Salad

Serves 5

PARVE

Ingredients:

3 long cucumbers (approx.
 1 lb)
1 clove of garlic
A small piece of fresh ginger
Chopped fresh mint or celery
 leaves
1 tbs coarse salt
¾-1 cup vinegar
1 tsp sugar

Directions:

Peel the cucumbers and cut in fine slices.

Sprinkle with coarse salt and allow to stand for 10 min.

Combine cucumbers with chopped ginger, and mint or celery leaves and put in a large jar.

Mix vinegar and sugar and pour over cucumbers.

Chilled cucumber salad keeps well for days.

Pesach

Matza Kugel

Matza Cake

Serves 4-5

Ingredients:

5 matzas
½ cup melted parve
   margarine
5 eggs
3 apples, grated
½ cup raisins
½ cup brown sugar
½ tsp salt
½ tsp cinnamon
½ tsp vanilla

Directions:

Soak the matzas in water for 15 minutes, then crumble them.

Mix all ingredients together and put in a greased cake dish.

Brush with 1 tsp of the melted margarine on top and bake in a preheated oven at 200°C (400°F) for 45-50 minutes.

Optional:
Coarsely grate 3-4 carrots and use instead of apples.
See also Hannemor's Lokshen, page 124.

"Kugel" is suitable as a side dish or as a snack with a cup of tea or coffee.

Matza Lasagna

Serves 6

MEAT

Ingredients:

2-3 tbs oil
2 large onions
1 kg (2 lbs) ground meat
  (veal or beef)
1 bunch parsley
1 garlic clove
1 carrot
½ tsp ginger
1 tsp paprika
1 tsp pepper
2 tbs tomato purée
½ cup bouillon
½ cup white wine
1 green pepper
1 red pepper
2 large tomatoes
6 matzas
2-3 stalks celery (inner
  stalks)

Sauce for topping:

1 cup bouillon
¼ cup white wine
Salt and pepper
1 tbs potato flour

> **Potato flour is used to thicken the sauce, as regular flour may not be used for Pesach.**

Directions:

Chop onion finely and fry in oil until golden.

Add meat and stir to separate.

Add crushed garlic and washed, chopped parsley.

Grate carrot on coarse side of grater and add to sauce.

Combine ginger, paprika, pepper, tomato purée, bouillon and white wine, and stir into sauce.

Let simmer for 10 minutes.

Grease a small baking pan or square oven-proof dish with a little margarine or oil.

Pour ⅓ of meat sauce over the bottom.

Rinse 3 matzas (do not soak) and place on sauce.

Add the next ⅓ of sauce.

Cut the peppers in rings and arrange on the meat sauce.

Add another layer of matzas.

Garnish with more peppers, sliced tomatoes and finely chopped celery.

To make the sauce for topping:

Heat the bouillon with wine, pepper and salt (if needed).

Stir potato flour in a little water and pour into sauce while stirring.

Remove from heat. Pour sauce over the lasagna and bake in a 220°C (425°F) oven for 30-35 minutes.

PARVE

Pesach Brownies
Makes about 50-60 pieces

Ingredients:
250 g (10 oz) margarine
350 g (14 oz) baking
  chocolate
2 cups matza meal
2¼ cups sugar
1 pinch of salt
1 tsp vanilla
2 tsp baking powder
8 eggs
1 cup chopped hazelnuts

Serve in decorative paper cupcake cups.

Directions:
Melt margarine and chocolate in a bowl over a pan of boiling water (or in a double boiler).

Combine matza meal, salt, vanilla, baking powder and nuts.

Beat eggs and sugar until light and fluffy.

Pour margarine and chocolate into the egg and sugar mixture. Beat together. Add the dry ingredients.

Pour the batter onto a greased 12"-15" baking tray. Bake in a preheated oven at 180°C (350°F) for 40 min.

Cut brownies in small squares when cold.

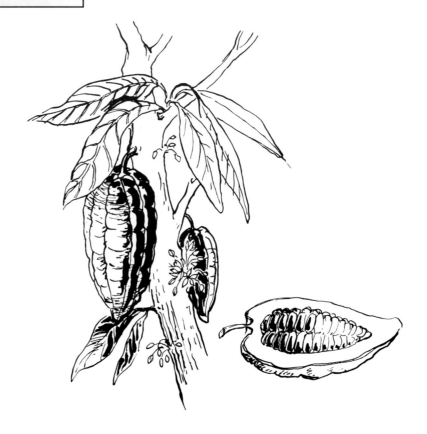

Carrot Cake for Pesach

Use a 9" × 13" baking tray

PARVE

Ingredients:
½ cup brown sugar
3 tbs oil
6 eggs
Grated rind and juice of
  1 orange
1 cup chopped nuts
¾ cup raisins
2 tsp vanilla
1 cup matza meal
¾ cup potato flour
1 tsp baking powder
400 g (1 lb) carrots

Optional:
½ cup chopped dates

Variation:
**Instead of vanilla, a
mixture of other aromatic
spices can be used
For example:
½ tsp ground cloves
1 tsp cardamom**

Directions:
Beat sugar and oil well.

Add eggs one at a time and beat in between.

Sprinkle grated orange rind together with juice on mixture.

Combine nuts, raisins, vanilla, matza meal, potato flour and baking powder and add to mixture.

Wash and grate the carrots (on the fine side of the grater). Add to other ingredients, together with chopped dates, if desired.

Mix all of these together thoroughly.

Pour the dough into a greased baking tray.

Bake in a preheated oven at 200°C (400°F) for 40 min.

The cake should be crisp on top and moist inside.

PARVE

Hannemor's Lokshen

Matza Cake

Serves 8-10

Ingredients:

5 matzas
8 eggs
1¼ cups brown sugar
½ cup raisins
½ cup chopped, blanched
  almonds
Juice and grated rind of
  1 lemon
¼ cup matza meal
¼ tsp salt

Directions:

Soak matzas in water for 15 min.

Break up, and press free of liquid.

Mix together all ingredients and pour into a greased oven-proof dish or bowl.

Bake in preheated oven at 170°C (350°F) for 1 hour.

Can be served with apple purée.

Pesach Layer Cake
Serves 8

PARVE

Ingredients:
6 eggs
1 cup sugar
¼ cup water
½ tsp grated lemon rind
2 tbs lemon juice
½ cup potato flour
½ cup cake meal
1 pinch of salt

Optional:
1 cup chopped almonds

Filling:
Approx. 2 cups fruit purée

Topping:
100 g (4 oz) chocolate
1 tbs parve margarine

Directions:
Beat egg yolks and sugar until light and fluffy. Add water, salt, lemon juice and rind.

Beat egg whites separately until stiff and fold carefully into mixture.

Combine cake meal, potato flour and finely chopped almonds. Sprinkle a little at a time into egg mixture.

Pour the dough into a springform pan and bake in oven at 170°C (350°F) for 1 hour.

When cake is cool, cut it into 2 layers. Spread fruit purée on bottom layer. Cover with top half.

Melt chocolate and margarine together. Spread over cake and decorate with fruit.

PARVE

Copenhagen Dessert Eggs
Makes 35-50 eggs

Ingredients:

Dough:
2 matzas
2 cups matza meal
150 g (6 oz) margarine,
  softened
¾ cup sugar
3 eggs
1 tbs grated lemon rind
1 tsp vanilla
1 cup almonds, finely
  ground

Filling:
1 apple
¾ cup raisins
1 cup almonds
1 tsp grated lemon rind
2 tbs brown sugar
1 tsp cinnamon, if desired

Coating:
1 egg white
About ½ cup matza meal

For frying:
1½ liters (1½ quarts) oil
  (can be reused)

Serve warm with cold apple purée!

Directions:

Soak the 2 matzas in cold water for 10-15 min.

Break up matzas and press out the water.

Mix soaked and pressed matzas with all dough ingredients.

Allow to chill for ½ an hour.

Meanwhile, prepare filling:

Peel, core and dice apple into small pieces.

Coarsely chop raisins and almonds.

Mix all ingredients for filling in a separate bowl.

Form the chilled dough in balls the size of a table tennis ball (work with moist hands to avoid its sticking to fingers).

Press the dough into an oval shape flat in the palm of your hand and put a tea spoon of the filling in the middle.

Close around the middle carefully and form an oblong egg.

Smooth the dough with moist hands, closing the dough completely around the filling.

Brush them with slightly beaten egg white.

Roll in matza meal and fry in hot oil 180°C (350°F) 5-6 balls at a time for about 6-7 minutes until golden brown in color.

Remove from oil and place on paper towels to absorb oil.

Step-by-Step

"Copenhagen Dessert Eggs" mean something special to me, as they remind me of my first years in Denmark. "Copenhagen Dessert Eggs" are a fine old Danish Jewish specialty that we ate at my in-law's home at each Seder. We looked forward to this dessert with anticipation every year.

I found part of the recipe in a very old hand-written book which belonged to my mother-in-law's Aunt Sus. The rest of it I had to try and guess. I hope that the younger generations will care to keep the tradition of these "Copenhagen Dessert Eggs" alive, even though it demands patience and love to prepare them correctly.

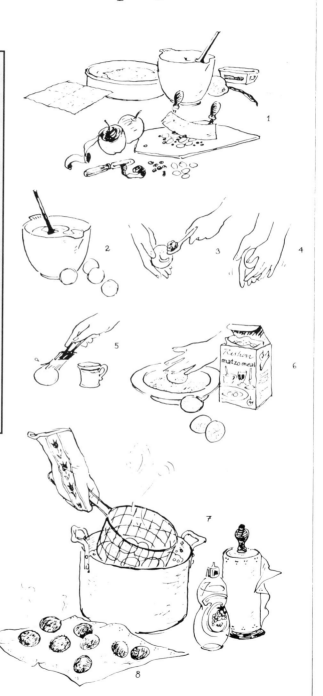

PARVE

Pesach Chocolate Cake
Serves 8-10

Ingredients:
200 g (8 oz) margarine
200 g (8 oz) dark cooking
  chocolate (parve)
4 eggs
¾ cup sugar
1 tsp vanilla
2 tbs brandy
1 cup potato flour
1 tsp baking powder

Filling:
Apricot jam

Garnish:
Chocolate or powdered
  sugar

Directions:
Grease a springform pan and sprinkle with matza meal.

Melt chocolate over a pan of hot water (or in a double boiler).

Beat margarine with vanilla and half the sugar.

Add to the melted chocolate.

Add egg yolks, one at a time. Beat well after each one is added. Combine potato flour and baking powder.

Sift flour, using strainer, into chocolate mixture together with brandy.

Beat egg whites stiff. Add remaining sugar and beat again for a minute. Fold into batter.

Pour batter into pan and and bake in a preheated oven for 180°C (350°F) for 40 minuts.

Allow cake to cool completely before taking it out of baking pan.

Cut cake into 2 layers.

Spread apricot jam between layers.

Garnish with melted chocolate or sifted powdered sugar.

"If I forget Thee, oh Jerusalem..."
Psalms, Chapter 137, Verse 5

Iyar

Iyar (April/May) is the month between two important holidays: Pesach (the exodus from Egypt) and Shavuot (the giving of the Torah).

Iyar has 3 days of celebration:

Yom Ha'atzmaut,

Israel Independence Day on the 5th of Iyar. It was on this date in the year 5708 (equivalent to May 14, 1948) that Israel was proclaimed an independent state.

Lag Ba'Omer,

The 18th of Iyar or the 33rd day of the counting of the Omer, which is in the 7 week period between the second day of Pesach and Shavuot. Due to a plague raging amongst the pupils of Rabbi Akiva in the year 135 B.C., these 7 weeks were declared a partial mourning period. However, on the 33rd day the plague halted. This day, therefore, became an exception from the mourning period. Today, Lag Ba'Omer is a general holiday. Families go on picnics in the park or forest and eat at bonfires.

Happy events, such as weddings, are permitted to be celebrated on this day.

Yom Yerushalayim,

The 28th of Iyar, Jerusalem Day. From 1948, Jerusalem was divided into two separate parts. After the Six Day War in June 1967, Jerusalem was reunited and became one big beautiful city!

For these three holidays, there are no special dishes or menus. However, because of the season, many wonderful spring fruits and vegetables are available. They inspire me to prepare an exciting menu of avocado, eggplant, coq au vin (chicken in wine), and for dessert, Jerusalem Chocolate Roll and Israeli strawberries or melons with a glass of fine Israeli wine.

With this we say *L'chaim*, which means: *To life, and to its pleasures!*

Eggplant in Tomato Sauce
Serves 6

PARVE

Ingredients:
2 large eggplants
1 egg
Matza meal or bread crumbs
Oil for frying eggplant

Sauce:
2 tbs olive oil
1 onion
2 cloves of garlic
½ cup chopped parsley
3-4 ripe tomatoes
1 small can (½ cup) tomato
  purée
Salt and pepper, to taste

Garnish:
Fresh red and green peppers

PARVE

*Avocado is another Israeli
crop in season for Yom
Ha'atzmaut.
Avocado is delicious:
1. Served plain with a
dribble of olive oil and a
dash of salt.
2. Mashed, with
hard-boiled eggs, grated
onions, lemon juice and a
drop of mayonnaise.
3. Cut in half and filled
with tuna salad (see next
recipe).*

Directions:
Slice the eggplant in 1 cm (½ inch) thick slices.

Sprinkle coarse salt on them, and allow to stand for ½ an hour. Rinse and dry.

Coat eggplant slices, first with egg and then with matza meal or bread crumbs.

Fry until brown in hot oil or margarine. They absorb quite a lot of oil. Place on paper towels to remove excess oil.

Meanwhile, prepare sauce.

Peel and slice onion in thin rings. Fry in hot olive oil together with crushed garlic.

Add parsley. Then add diced tomatoes and tomato purée.

Cover the sauce and allow to simmer for 10 minutes. Add salt and pepper according to taste.

Arrange eggplant in an oven-proof dish and warm in oven. Pour the warm sauce on top and garnish with pepper rings just before serving.

Spring Tuna Salad

Serves 6-8

Ingredients:
2 cans of tuna fish in oil
approx. 300 g (12 oz)
1 can (280 g [11 oz]) of corn
1 can (280 g [11 oz])
asparagus pieces
3–4 tbs of mayonnaise
Juice of ½ lemon
Salt and white pepper

Garnish:
2 hard-boiled eggs
Parsley

Directions:
Mix 2-3 tbs of liquid from asparagus can with mayonnaise, lemon juice, pepper and salt.

Press the oil out of the tuna fish with a fork. Drain the corn and asparagus from the liquid in the can.

Mix tuna and vegetables into the mayonnaise dressing.

Add salt if necessary.

Garnish with wedges or slices of hard-boiled eggs and parsley. In order to get the best taste from this salad, it is important that the tuna, corn and asparagus are good quality.

Mousse with Tuna and Capers

Serves 8

Ingredients:
2 cans of tuna fish in oil
approx. 300 g (12 oz)
1 cup sour cream
2 tbs lemon juice
¼ cup capers
1 tsp curry powder
1 tsp basil
14 g (½ oz) Kosher gelatin
powder (see pg 12)
¼ liter (1 cup) whipping
cream
Salt
1 tsp white pepper

Garnish:
Endive leaves
Tomatoes (slices or wedges)
Lemon slices

Directions:
Chop the tuna fish in a chopper, together with the capers. Put in a bowl and add lemon juice, sour cream and spices.

Soak the gelatin powder in ¼ cup water in a heat-proof bowl for 10 min. Then place bowl in a pot of water and heat water up to boil. The gelatin will dissolve and become transparent. Gradually trickle the gelatin into the bowl of other ingredients and beat with an electric mixer in order to avoid lumps.

Whip the cream and fold in carefully. Rinse a ring mold with cold water, put in the tuna and shake the ring to settle tuna mousse.

Cover with foil and refrigerate to chill and jell.

When serving, loosen the sides with a sharp knife. Dip the mould in a bowl of hot water and invert onto a serving plate. Garnish with endive leaves, lemon slices and cut tomatoes.

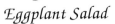

Baba Ghanoush

Eggplant Salad

Serves 6-8

PARVE

Ingredients:

3 eggplants
3 tbs mayonnaise or tehina
  paste
3 crushed cloves of garlic
Salt and white pepper
Juice of 2 lemons
3 tbs of chopped parsley

Optional:

½ tsp cayenne pepper

Garnish

Olives
Chopped parsley
Lemon slices

Directions:

Wash and wipe eggplant. Prick the skins with a fork in 3-4 places.

Put eggplants on foil in a hot oven (250°C / 470°F) for 30-40 minutes, until the skin gets dark and wrinkled.

Take out of oven and slit the eggplant.

Scrape the pulp out of the skins with a spoon onto a plate – discard juice and skin and allow eggplant to cool.

Put pulp together with remaining ingredients in a chopper or blender and blend for 1 minute (can also be mashed with a fork).

Garnish with chopped parsley, lemon slices and olives.

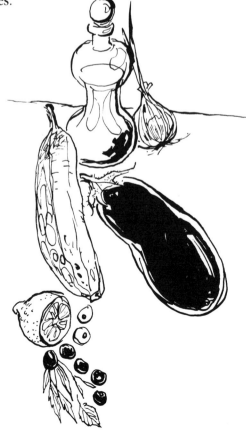

Turkish Salad

Serves 8

PARVE

Ingredients:
4 tbs olive oil
2 large onions
2 fresh yellow peppers
3 fresh green peppers
3 fresh red peppers
4 fresh tomatoes
50 g (2 oz) olives (pitted)
1 tsp thyme
Salt and pepper
$\frac{1}{2}$ tsp cumin
3 tbs tomato purée
$\frac{1}{2}$ tsp cayenne pepper

Garnish:
Juice of 1 lemon
4 tbs chopped parsley
Lemon slices

Directions:

Peel and chop onions. Fry in hot oil until transparent.

Finely dice fresh peppers and add them to the onion.

Sauté for 3-4 minutes.

Dice the tomatoes and olives and add them.

Add spices and tomato purée, cover and allow to simmer for 10-15 min.

Just before serving, add lemon juice, chopped parsley and garnish with slices of lemon.

Serve hot or cold.

Moroccan Carrot Salad

Serves 8-10

PARVE

Ingredients:

1 kg (2 lbs) carrots
3-4 cloves of garlic, crushed
½ cup olive oil
1 tsp Dijon mustard or
    mustard powder
½ tsp cayenne pepper
½ tsp cumin
½ tsp salt
½ tsp pepper
Juice of 2-3 lemons
3 tbs chopped parsley

Directions:

Wash and scrub the carrots.

Put in a large pot. Cover with cold water and boil for 15 minutes (they have to be firm).

Remove and allow to cool. Then, cut into 1 cm (½") thick slices.

Mix all the remaining ingredients into a dressing and pour over carrots.

One can add more of the spices, according to taste.

A delicious piquant salad which is very popular in Israel, and tastes best when a day old.

Asparagus Galil

Serves 4

PARVE

Ingredients:

1 can of long green
 asparagus
2 ripe avocados
2 hard-boiled eggs
1 tbs lemon juice
Salt and pepper, to taste

Garnish:

Slices of lime
Green olives
Fresh red pepper

Directions:

Put asparagus in a colander and allow to drain.

Arrange in 4 serving plates.

Mash pulp of avocados with eggs.

Add lemon juice, salt and pepper.

Spoon avocado mixture over asparagus and garnish
with lime, olives and a ring of red pepper.

MEAT

Chicken in Herbed Marinade
Serves 4

Ingredients:
1 large chicken

Marinade:
¾ cup olive oil
5-6 tbs lime juice
1 crushed clove of garlic
1 small onion, finely chopped
1 bay leaf
1 tbs parsley, finely chopped
1 tbs dill, finely chopped
Salt and pepper

Directions:
Cut the chicken in desired amount of pieces.

Put in a bowl or glass dish. Mix marinade ingredients and pour over chicken. Allow to chill for 2-3 hours.

Then, dry pieces of chicken with paper towels to remove excess marinade. Fry in hot olive oil.

Arrange in oven-proof dish. Strain marinade over chicken.

Cover with foil and bake in a warm oven at 200°C (400°F) for 1 hour.

Serve with rice with fresh herbs (see following recipe).

Rice with Fresh Herbs

Serves 4

MEAT

Ingredients:
2 cups rice
2 tbs oil
2 tbs parsley, finely chopped
2 tbs dill, finely chopped
2 tbs chives, finely chopped
1 tsp salt
3 cups water

Optional :
1 cup green peas
1 chicken

Directions:
Wash rice with cold water and strain.

Heat oil in a pot.

Put in the rice and fry for 2-3 minutes, stirring continuously.

Add the herbs and stir again.

Pour water on rice.

Stir and cover.

Allow rice to boil and then simmer for about 15 minutes.

Just before serving, loosen rice with a fork.

Add, if desired, the green peas.

Serve with Chicken in Herbed Marinade and chilled, peeled cucumber, cut into long sticks.

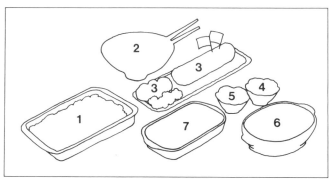

Iyar

Chicken in Wine

Serves 6

Ingredients:

2 kg (4 lbs) large chicken
¾ cup dry white wine
1 clove of garlic, crushed
1 tsp oregano
1 tbs parsley, finely chopped
Salt and pepper
½ cup olive oil
250 g (½ lb) mushrooms
2 tbs parve margarine

Picnic Basket:
Traditionally Lag Ba'omer is picnic day in the forest or park, together with family and friends.
Sesame chicken and crispy green salad will suit the occasion perfectly.

Directions:

Cut the chicken in desired pieces.

Mix wine, garlic, oregano, parsley, salt, pepper and oil together in a large bowl.

Put in chicken pieces and cover with marinade.

Allow to chill for about 2 hours.

Heat margarine in a frying pan. Remove excess marinade from chicken pieces and fry them lightly brown on both sides.

Arrange chicken in an oven-proof dish.

Strain the marinade over the chicken.

Wash the mushrooms under cold running water and slice. Saute the mushrooms for a couple of minutes in the frying pan and pour over the chicken. Cover and bake in a warm oven at 200°C (400°F) for 40 minutes.

Serve with rice.

Sesame Chicken

Serves 4

Ingredients:

1½ kg (3 lb) large chicken
1 cup flour
1 cup sesame seeds
Salt and pepper
1 tsp curry powder
1 egg
½ cup water or broth
Parve margarine for frying
   chicken

Directions:

Combine flour, sesame seeds and spices in a brown paper or plastic bag. Divide chicken in desired pieces and put them in the bag to coat.

Mix egg and water or broth. Dip in the chicken pieces, covering both sides. Then dip again in the dry ingredients.

Heat the margarine and fry the chicken until golden brown in color.

Put in warm oven at 180°C (350°F) for about 40 min.

Serve with crispy salad.

Bamia Kuba

Meatballs in Okra

Serves 6

MEAT

Ingredients for sauce:

500 g (1 lb) okra
4 tbs oil
1 onion, diced
1 cup tomatoes, finely
  chopped
½ tsp salt
½ tsp turmeric
1 tsp pepper
1 clove of garlic, crushed
Juice of 1 lemon
1 tbs sugar

Ingredients for meatballs:

300 g (12 oz) ground meat
3 onions, grated
1 tbs chopped celery or mint
  leaves
½ tsp turmeric
½ tsp pepper
½ tsp salt
1 pinch ground cloves
¼ tsp cardamom
2 tbs matza meal
1 egg

Directions:

Wash and dry the okra. Trim the top.

Heat 2 tbs of oil in a pan and fry the okra 6-7 minutes to avoid it getting slimy.

Remove from heat and prepare sauce.

Heat 2 tbs of oil in a pot and fry the peeled and diced onion until lightly brown and add the garlic, stirring frequently.

Then add the turmeric, tomatoes, salt and pepper.

Put the okra in the sauce and add 1 cup water.

Bring the sauce to a boil and allow to simmer for 6-7 minutes.

Mix lemon juice and sugar and pour into the sauce.

Mix all the ingredients for the meatballs.

Form small meatballs with moist hands (to prevent sticking) and put in the simmering sauce.

Increase heat for the first 5 minutes and then return to a low heat for 15 minutes.

Serve with rice.

Okra:
Also known as "Lady Fingers", this 7-10 cm (3-4") long green pod is from the Hibiscus plant.
Okra tastes good in tomato sauce or as here, in a sweet and sour soup with meatballs. See also page 90-91.

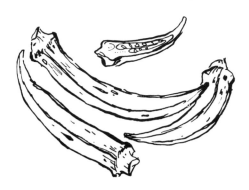

Veal Tongue in Wine and Vegetables

Serves 8

MEAT

Ingredients:

1½ kg (2-3 lbs) veal tongue
2 tbs olive oil
2 onions
2 carrots
½ cup dry kosher red wine
½ cup tomato purée
Salt and pepper
2 bay leaves
1 tsp thyme
3 tsp chopped parsley
3 fresh peppers in different
  colors
6 small tomatoes

If you choose to drink wine with the meal, the same wine as used in the sauce will suit best.

PARVE

Dessert:
A bowl of fresh strawberries is the perfect finish to this delicious meal.
Wash the strawberries thoroughly, but leave the green tops on for decoration!

Directions:

Put the tongue in a large pot and cover with water.

Cook for about 2½ hours until tender (or purchase a ready-boiled tongue at the butcher's).

Peel the skin off and cut the tongue in neat slices.

Arrange the slices in a deep oven-proof dish and prepare the sauce.

Heat the oil in a pot. Peel and cut onions in rings and slice carrots. Sauté them in the oil until onion becomes golden in color.

Mix wine and ¼ cup broth from cooked tongue and stir into sauce.

Stir frequently, adding the tomato purée and spices, and salt and pepper to taste.

Pour boiling water on tomatoes and skin them. Then add to sauce.

Allow sauce to simmer a couple of minutes. Pour the hot sauce over the slices of tongue.

Cut the fresh peppers in rings and arrange on top.

Warm the dish before serving.

Garnish with chopped parsley, and serve with small boiled potatoes sprinkled with dill.

Jerusalem Chocolate Roll

Serves 8

PARVE

Ingredients:

3 eggs
½ cup sugar
½ cup flour
½ cup potato flour
1 tsp baking powder
2 tbs cocoa
2 tbs water

Filling:

500 g (1 lb) fresh dates,
  pitted and chopped
1 cup chopped nuts
½ cup sweet wine
1 tsp cardamom
2 tbs apricot jam

Garnish:

100 g (4 oz) semi-sweet
  chocolate, melted with
  1 tbs margarine or
  powdered sugar

Directions:

Mix ingredients for filling and set aside.

Beat egg and sugar until light and fluffy.

Combine flour, potato flour, baking powder and cocoa and fold carefully into egg and sugar. Fold in water.

Spread the batter in a greased baking tray and bake in a preheated oven at 200°C (400°F) for 8-10 min.

Turn cake over onto a large baking paper sprinkled with powdered sugar.

Spread filling over the cake quickly and roll up tightly.

Wrap in baking paper and allow to cool.

Garnish with sifted powdered sugar or brush with melted chocolate.

Cochin "Bread"

Coconut and Rice Cake

Serves 10

DAIRY

Ingredients:

6 matzas
4 tbs parve margarine,
  softened
1½ cups brown sugar
1 cup rice flour
1 tsp baking powder
1 cup shredded coconut
½ tsp cardamom
½ cup raisins
1 cup milk
½ cup almonds
3 eggs

Directions:

Soak matzas in water for 15 min. Press free of liquid.

Mix margarine, matzas and sugar very well.

Add in the eggs one at a time, stirring between each one.

Combine rice flour, coconut, cardamom and raisins and add to matzas alternating with the milk.

Blanch and skin the almonds. Then chop and sprinkle into batter.

Pour the batter into a well-greased baking dish and bake in preheated oven at 250°C (450°F) for the first 10 min. Then, lower to 200°C (400°F) and continue baking for a further 50 min.

PARVE

It is possible to substitute milk with 1 cup fresh orange juice.

COCHIN
A coastal town in South India where Jews have been living since the year 1000. Many of the Cochin Jews moved to Bombay where I got to taste their exciting and exotic food.
As a child I often wondered with envy, if their bread tastes so good, how wonderful their cakes might taste. . .

"...Seven weeks shall you count for yourself... And you will keep the Feast of Weeks to the Lord your God..."

Deuteronomy, Chapter 16, Verses 9-10

Shavuot

Shavuot is celebrated on the 6th and 7th of *Sivan*, which falls in the late Spring, in May or June. From the end of Pesach until Shavuot, 49 days are counted. This period is called the **Counting of the Omer** (omer, in Hebrew, means a sheaf of wheat). At the end of this seven-week period, the first wheat is to be harvested, and the Feast of Shavuot is celebrated.

Two traditional names for this holiday are *Hag HaKatzir* – the holiday of the first wheat harvest, and *Hag HaBikurim* – holiday of the first fruits. Because the holiday concludes the seven-week counting of the Omer, it is also called *Atzeret*, or The Conclusion.

Shavuot is one of three traditional **pilgrimage holidays**, the other two being Sukkoth and Pesach. Shavuot was a time in ancient Israel when pilgrims went to the Temple with offerings of their first harvest. To this day, it is traditional to celebrate the day with brightly decorated baskets of fruit, sheaves of wheat and garlands of flowers for the children.

Shavuot is much more than a harvest festival, however: this is the day which marks the **giving of the Ten Commandments** to Moses on Mount Sinai during the exodus.

Counting the Omer has also been a way to introspect and prepare ourselves for this great event, occurring a mere 49 days after coming out of our Egyptian bondage.

Because the Ten Commandments form the basis for the Torah and for all Jewish law, this day celebrates a new beginning for the Jewish people – as one nation with its own identity.

This aspect of Shavuot has given the holiday its fourth name: *Zman Matan Torateinu*, which means the time of the giving of our Torah.

It is a tradition to eat **dairy foods** on Shavuot. One of the explanations for this is that when the commandments were first given to the ancient Jews, they did not fully understand the strict dietary regulations of kashrut. In order to avoid eating non-kosher foods, it is said that they avoided eating meat at first. Another explanation for this tradition is the connection of the Exodus and the journey to the Promised Land: *"From the misery of Egypt to a country abundant with milk and honey..."* (Exodus, Chapter 3, Verse 8-17)

On Shavuot, Jewish homes are decorated with flowers and greenery and family and friends gather for a festive meal of dairy foods, often including blintzes, cheesecake and fruit and vegetable specialties.

In Israel, harvest celebrations are held in many farming communities, the most colorful of them taking place on the *kibbutzim* (collective farms).

DAIRY

Curd Cheese

Homemade Cream Cheese

Serves 8-10

Ingredients:

1 sour milk product (sour cream, buttermilk, leben, etc.)

Most cheeses contain rennet, an animal-derived enzyme used to coagulate the milk and separate the whey.

This poses a problem in a kosher household. Some cheeses are made with synthetic or bacterial enzymes and are therefore kosher (check for kosher supervision/certificate). Homemade curd cheese is a good solution and can be made easily. It can be used in the following recipes or enjoyed plain on a piece of rye bread with a dash of salt and pepper.

Curd cheese is similar to a lean cream cheese.

To prepare:

If milk product is in a carton, place the unopened carton in a pot of water reaching up to $1/3$ of its height and boil water for a couple of minutes. If it is not in a carton, pour contents into in a thick-bottomed casserole and bring slowly to a boil.

Remove from heat and let cool.

Pour in a colander lined with a thin muslin cloth or coffee filter.

Leave covered to drain overnight in a cool place.

Herb Cheese

Serves 8-10

DAIRY

Ingredients:
450 g (1 lb) cream cheese
200 g (8 oz) butter, melted
Salt and white pepper
2 tbs chopped parsley
2 tbs chopped chives
2 tbs chopped dill

Optional:
1 clove of garlic, crushed

Garnish:
Lemon slices

DAIRY

Danish Summer Salad:
Combine cream cheese with
finely diced tomatoes,
cucumber, radishes, chives,
salt and pepper and, if
desired, a little
mayonnaise.
Serve with whole-grain or
rye bread.

Directions:
Whip the cream cheese with the butter, salt, pepper and garlic.

Add most of the chopped herbs and keep about $1/3$ for garnishing.

Roll the cheese in baking paper into a tight "sausage" and allow to chill for a couple of hours (it will become firm because of the butter).

Then roll the cheese in the remaining $1/3$ green herbs and garnish with slices of lemon.

Avocado Cheese

Approx. 1 liter (2 lbs)

Ingredients:
400 g (1 lb) cream cheese
125 g (6 oz) butter
1 tsp salt
½ tsp white pepper
1 clove of garlic, crushed
½ tsp cayenne pepper
1 tsp paprika
1 tbs chopped chives
1 tbs chopped parsley
3 ripe avocados
1 tsp lemon juice

Garnish:
Small radishes
A few stalks of celery leaves

Directions:
Melt butter and beat in the soft cheese.

Sprinkle in the chopped herbs and spices.

Mash the avocado pulp and mix in.

Add lemon juice.

Allow avocado cheese to chill in refrigerator for 2 hours before serving.

When serving, garnish with radishes, parsley or the tender stalks and leaves of celery.

Can also be used as a dip or spread.

French Onion Soup

Serves 6-8

DAIRY

Ingredients:

75 g (3 oz) butter
6 large onions
2 tbs flour
1½ liter (6 cups) vegetable
   stock
½ tsp white pepper
2 bay leaves
Salt, to taste
6 slices of white bread
6 tbs grated mozzarella or
   cheddar cheese

French onion soup is usually made with a good strong meat stock as a base.
Since in its original form it also contains cheese, in a kosher home we have to substitute the meat stock with vegetable stock (homemade or from kosher vegetable soup mix).
Remember, when a mix is used, seasoning with salt is unnecessary.

Directions:

Peel and cut onions in thin rings.

Melt butter in a pot.

Add onion, sauté over low heat while stirring well, until the onion gets transparent (about 10 minutes).

Add the flour. Keep stirring for a couple of minutes until the flour turns a golden color.

Pour in the vegetable stock, stir well and add the pepper and bay leaves.

Allow soup to simmer over low heat for 25-30 minutes. Until this point in the preparations, the onion soup can be made in advance.

Toast the slices of white bread and dice into small squares.

Remove the bay leaves from the soup.

Pour the soup into heat-proof soup bowls.

Drop in the bread cubes and cover with 1 tablespoon of grated cheese.

Place the bowls in a preheated oven at 220°C (450°F) and leave them in until the cheese melts.

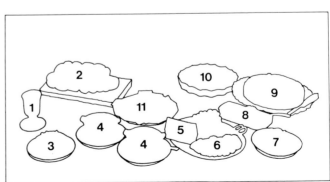

Shavuot

PARVE

Gazpacho
Chilled Tomato Soup
Serves 6

Ingredients:
½ lb cucumbers
1 onion
2 cloves of garlic
1 fresh green pepper
1 kg (2 lbs) ripe tomatoes
2 slices of stale white bread,
   toasted
¼ cup olive oil
¼ cup vinegar
1 tsp salt
½ tsp pepper
1 pinch cayenne pepper
1 cup water

Garnish:
1 fresh green pepper
2 onions
½ cucumber

Directions:
Pour boiling water on the tomatoes and skin them.

Cut cucumber, onion, garlic, green peppers, tomatoes and bread and put into a blender or food processor and blend.

Add olive oil, vinegar, salt and pepper.

The soup should be thick and yet fluid.

Gazpacho can keep up to one whole week in the refrigerator because of the vinegar.

Cut the garnish in small pieces and serve with soup.

Gazpacho:
A chilled Spanish summer soup that can easily make a whole meal, accompanied by warm baguettes.

Mushroom Pâté

Serves 6-8

DAIRY

Ingredients:
4 tbs butter
500 g (1 lb) mushrooms
200 g (8 oz) onion
1 cup chopped hazelnuts
3 cloves of garlic, crushed
3 eggs
1½ cups whipping cream
½ tsp salt
1 tsp pepper
1½ cups matza meal or
    bread crumbs
2 tbs fresh thyme
3 tbs chopped parsley

Garnish:
Tomato wedges
Watercress

Directions:
Peel and chop onions in small pieces. Sauté in melted butter until transparent.

Add the garlic, salt and pepper.

Rinse and chop mushrooms coarsely.

Sauté them with the onions for 5-6 minutes. Remove from heat and allow to cool.

Add chopped hazelnuts to the sauce.

Add matza meal or bread crumbs, parsley and thyme.

Beat eggs and cream together and mix with the other ingredients.

Pour the mixture into a well-greased soufflé dish, and bake in a preheated oven at 175°C (350°F) for 45 minutes.

Can be served warm or cold.

MEAT

Stuffed Artichoke Hearts
Serves 4

Ingredients:
300 g (12 oz) ground meat
1 egg
1 slice bread or ½ matza
1 tsp soup mix (meat or
    vegetable)
½ tsp ground cloves
1 tsp pepper
1 tsp ground ginger
12-15 artichoke hearts
    (canned or frozen)
3 fresh leeks
1 tbs parve margarine
    (to grease the dish)
1 cup meat or vegetable
    stock
½ tsp thyme
1 tsp white pepper
Salt, if desired

Garnish:
15-20 stuffed olives
A few sprigs of parsley

Directions:
Mix together ground meat, egg, soaked and pressed bread or matza, soup mix, cloves, ginger and pepper.

Grease an oven-proof dish with margarine.

Wash and thinly slice the leeks in rings. Spread them in the bottom of the dish. Add thyme and pepper (and salt, if desired) and stock.

Cover the dish and place in a preheated oven at 200°C (400°F) for 15 minutes.

Take out the dish. Top the artichoke hearts with the meat mixture and place them over the leeks.

Return the dish to the oven and bake uncovered for 15-20 minutes.

Garnish each artichoke with a stuffed olive and a small sprig of parsley.

Baked Fish with Mushrooms and Wine

Serves 6

DAIRY

Ingredients:

12 fillets of plaice or sole
4 tbs lemon juice
Salt and white pepper
1 cup dry white wine
60 g (2 oz) butter
500 g (1 lb) mushrooms
A few sprigs of dill

PARVE

Potatoes:
Small parboiled potatoes
will suit this dish very well.
They can be boiled and
peeled in advance, and just
warmed up before serving
as follows:
Put the potatoes in a pot,
cover with cold water and 1
teaspoon salt. Bring slowly
to a boil.
Drain and serve warm,
garnished with fresh dill.

Directions:

Grease an oven-proof dish with a little butter.

Wash and dry the fish fillets.

Sprinkle with salt and lemon juice. Roll up each fillet with a sprig of dill inside.

Arrange the rolled fillets in the dish close to one another with the edge facing downwards.

Rinse and clean the mushrooms. Slice thinly and sauté in butter for about 4-5 minutes. Add a little salt and white pepper. Pour over the rolled fillets.

Add white wine. Cover with foil and put the dish in a preheated oven at 200°C (400°F) for 20 minutes.

Quiche

Makes 2 pies

Ingredients:

Crust:

2½ cups flour

200 g (8 oz) margarine or
   butter, chilled

1 egg

1 tsp salt

¼ cup cold water

Fillings:

**1. Onion and Tuna or
   Salmon:**

3 onions

200 g (8 oz) tuna or salmon
   (approx. 1 can)

1 tbs vegetable or onion
   soup mix

1 tbs margarine

½ cup water

3 eggs

1 cup sour cream

2. Mushroom:

Substitute tuna and onion
   with 500 g (1 lb) cleaned
   and diced mushrooms.

Instead of onion soup
   powder, use mushroom
   soup powder

Garnish:

Tomatoes

Red/green/yellow bell
   peppers

Dill

1 tbs grated mozzarella
   cheese

Directions:

Crust:

Chop the cold margarine into the flour and salt,
using a knife or a pastry cutter.

Add egg and cold water. Gather together (carefully
by hand) into a soft but not sticky pastry.

Pack in foil and allow to chill for ½ an hour.

Grease a flan tin (8-9" diameter) with a little
margarine. Line the bottom and sides with the
chilled pastry (the portion is enough for 2 flan tins).

Prick with a fork in 3-4 places and bake in a
preheated oven at 200°C (400°F) for 10 minutes.

Filling:

Melt the margarine or butter in a pot.

Peel and slice the onions in rings and sauté in the
melted margarine.

Add tuna (if salmon is used, check for tiny bones).
Then add soup powder and stir well. Add water and
allow to simmer for 5 minutes.

Remove from heat and cool.

Beat together sour cream and eggs.

On the baked flan, first spread the tuna and onion
or mushroom filling evenly. Then pour the egg and
cream mixture on top.

Garnish with slices of tomatoes, fresh
red/green/yellow peppers, dill and grated chees.

Return the flan to oven and bake for 30 minutes at
200°C (400°F).

Serve with a crispy green salad and wholegrain
bread.

Marinated Turkey with Spinach

Serves 6

MEAT

Ingredients:

1 kg (2 lbs) turkey breast
(approx. 12 thin slices)
½ cup olive oil
½ cup white wine
3 whole cloves
3 bay leaves
1 clove of garlic, crushed
Juice of ½ lemon
3 tbs chopped herbs (dill,
parsley, chives, etc.)
1 tsp salt
½ tsp white pepper
1 chopped onion
250 g (½ lb) frozen spinach
Salt and pepper
1 tsp ground nutmeg

> **You will need very thin slices of turkey breast. It is easier to have the butcher do the slicing, if possible.**

> **This dish is good with boiled saffron rice sprinkled with green herbs**

Directions:

Cut the turkey breast in thin slices or use pre-sliced breast from the butcher.

Place the meat in a deep dish or bowl.

Mix olive oil, white wine, cloves, bay leaves, garlic, lemon juice, herbs, 1 tsp salt, white pepper and onion together into a marinade and pour over the turkey pieces.

Chill for a couple of hours.

Thaw the spinach and press out any liquid.

Season the spinach with salt, pepper and nutmeg.

Put a tablespoon of spinach on each turkey slice.

Roll each slice tightly and place in an oven-proof dish with the edges facing downwards.

Strain the marinade and pour over the rolled slices.

Bake in a preheated oven at 200°C (400°F) for 25 minutes.

Cheesecake

Serves 10-12

Ingredients:

Pastry:
1¼ cups flour
4 tbs margarine or butter
¼ cup sugar
1 small egg

Filling:
650 g (1½ lbs) cream cheese
4 tbs flour
4 eggs
¾ cup sugar
1 pinch of salt
1 tsp grated lemon rind
1 tbs lemon juice
1 tsp vanilla
1 cup whipping cream

Optional:
Garnish cheesecake with
  fresh fruit.

Directions:

Combine pastry ingredients and mix together lightly. Allow to chill for ½ an hour.

Line the bottom of a springform pan with the dough.

Filling:

Beat egg yolks very well with sugar.

Add lemon juice, grated lemon rind, salt and vanilla.

Mix cheese with flour and add to egg and sugar mixture.

Whip cream to soft peaks and fold into mixture.

Beat egg whites until stiff and fold into mixture carefully.

Pour onto the pastry and smooth the top.

Bake in a preheated oven at 200°C (400°F) for 50 minutes.

Turn off the heat and allow cake to cool in the oven.

Cheese and Nut Roll

Serves 6-8

DAIRY

Ingredients:

450 g (1 lb) lowfat cream
  cheese
200 g (8 oz) butter, melted
½ cup sour cream
1 tbs sugar
1 tsp vanilla
1 tbs concentrated orange
  juice (can be frozen)
2 cups chopped nuts
  (walnuts, hazelnuts,
  almonds)

Optional:

1 tbs brandy or orange
  liqueur

Garnish:

Nuts and orange slices

DAIRY

Variation:
*Nut cheese on small
biscuits: Small cheese balls
rolled in chopped nuts and
placed on small biscuits
make great snacks at
receptions.*

Directions:

Beat well: cream cheese, melted butter, sour cream, vanilla, sugar, concentrated orange juice, ²/₃ of the chopped nuts and, if desired, brandy or liqueur.

In baking paper, roll the cheese into a sausage. Allow to chill for a couple of hours.

Take out and roll in remaining chopped nuts and place on serving plate.

Garnish with nuts and thin slices of orange.

Blintzes

Stuffed Crepes

Makes 10-12

Ingredients:
Batter:
¾ cup flour
¼ tsp salt
1 tbs sugar
3 eggs
1 cup milk
½ tsp vanilla
Butter or margarine for
*   frying pancakes*

Filling:
200 g (8 oz) cream cheese
1 egg yolk
1 tsp sugar
½ tsp vanilla
1 tbs concentrated orange
*   juice*

Optional
½ cup currants or raisins

Directions:

Mix ingredients for filling and set aside.

Beat all ingredients for batter.

Heat a little margarine or butter in a flat pan.

Pour a little batter (approx. 2-3 tbs) on the hot pan and fry pancakes light brown – only on one side.

Turn over to a greased plate – fried side upwards.

Put 1 tablespoon of filling in the middle and fold the sides over the middle making a rectangle.

Arrange the blintzes in a greased oven-proof dish.

Pour a little melted margarine or butter on the blintzes and warm in the oven at 170°C (350°F) for 10-15 min.

Serve warm with cold sour cream.

Variation:
Warm blintzes served with cold Orange Parfait (see page 162).
Tastes wonderful !

Orange Mousse
Serves 8

Ingredients:
2 envelopes of kosher gelatin
powder, each 14 g (½ oz)
(see page 12)
1 cup frozen concentrated
orange juice
½ cup sugar
1 tsp grated orange rind
2 cups (1 pint) whipping
cream

Garnish:
Fresh strawberries
Orange slices

Directions:
Sprinkle gelatin into ½ cup cold water to soften for 10 minutes.

Mix orange juice, sugar and ¼ cup water and heat until sugar melts.

Add gelatin and stir until it dissolves.

Allow to cool until it reaches a syrup-like consistency.

Add the orange rind.

Whip the cream until stiff and add the orange juice. Whisk well.

Pour the mousse into a rinsed ring mold and allow to gel in the fridge.

When serving:
Dip the mold in warm water, loosen the sides with a sharp knife and invert on a serving dish.

Fill the middle with fresh strawberries and garnish outer ring with orange slices.

Coffee Parfait

Serves 8-10

Ingredients:

5 egg yolks
¾ cup sugar
3 tsp instant coffee
1 tbs coffee liqueur
2 cups whipping cream,
    whipped
½ tsp almond oil

Garnish:

Coffee beans or instant
    coffee

Directions:

Dissolve coffee in 1 cup boiling water.

Stir well and allow to cool completely.

Beat egg yolks and sugar until light and fluffy.

Add coffee and coffee liqueur.

Fold in whipped cream.

Brush an ice cream mold with a little almond oil.

Pour parfait into mold and place in freezer.

Stir the parfait every 20 minutes for the first 2 hours, to keep the coffee from sinking to the bottom.

When serving, unmold by dipping mold in a bowl of hot water and inverting onto a serving plate.

Garnish with coffee beans or ground coffee.

Orange Parfait

Serves 8-10

Ingredients:

4 egg yolks
½ cup sugar
Grated rind of ½ orange
½ cup frozen concentrated
    orange juice
1 tbs orange liqueur
50 g (2 oz) semi-sweet
    chocolate
½ cup chopped nuts
2 cups (1 pint) whipping
    cream
2 egg whites
½ tsp almond oil

Garnish:

Grated chocolate
Orange slices

Directions:

Beat egg yolks and sugar until light and fluffy.

Add orange rind, orange juice and liqueur.

Chop the chocolates and nuts and add to mixture.

Whip the cream and egg whites stiff – each separately.

First fold in the whipped cream, then fold in stiff egg whites.

Pour into an ice cream mold, greased with almond oil.

Cover and allow to freeze.

When serving, unmold and garnish.

Danish Crackers

Makes 25-30

PARVE

Ingredients:

3 cups flour
4 tbs soft parve margarine
1 tbs oil
1 tsp salt
25 g (1 oz) fresh yeast
½ cup lukewarm water
2 tbs mixture of different
  seeds and grains (whole
  wheat, sesame, flax,
  poppyseed, rye)

Garnish:

Egg
2-3 tbs seeds (poppy seeds,
  flax, sesame, sunflower
  seeds)

Directions:

Combine flour, margarine, oil, salt and 2 tbs seeds and grains.

Dissolve yeast in lukewarm water and add to flour mixture.

Knead together into a soft dough.

Roll out dough very flat onto a floured board.

Cut the dough into rectangles.

Brush with beaten egg and sprinkle with seeds. Press the seeds into the dough.

Place the biscuits on a baking tray covered with baking paper.

Bake in preheated oven at 220°C (450°F) for 10-12 minutes, or until light brown in color.

In recent years, it has become very popular to bake your own wholegrain bread. In Denmark, we get a variety of ready-mixed coarse flour and seeds like flax, poppyseeds, sesame and sunflower seeds. Of course, there are also rye and other flours for a wide variety of possibilities.

Spinach and Tuna Pâté

Serves 4

Ingredients:

2 tbs butter

1 leek (or onion)

250 g (½ lb) frozen spinach

4 tbs chopped green herbs
(dill, parsley, chives)

2 cans of tuna (approx.
350 g [14 oz])

1 tsp salt

1 tsp pepper

½ cup matza meal

1 cup grated cheese

1 cup whipping cream

2 eggs

Directions:

Melt the butter in a pot.

Wash and slice the leek or onion in thin rings and sauté in butter. Add the thawed spinach and stir well.

Stir in the herbs and season with salt and pepper.

Add the tuna and allow to simmer for a couple of minutes.

Add the matza meal into the pot. Stir well and remove from heat. Allow to cool to lukewarm.

Grease an oven-proof dish with butter. Pour the tuna mixture into the dish and spread evenly.

Beat cream and egg together and pour over the dish. Garnish with grated cheese.

Bake in a preheated oven at 175°C (350°F) for 30 min.

Serve warm or cold with baguettes and salad.

Tammuz is one of the summer months in the Jewish calendar without any holiday. However, the 17th day of the month is a fast day to commemorate the fall of Jerusalem's outer wall which resulted in the destruction of the Second Temple in the year 70 C.E.

Spaghetti Squash

Serves 8

Ingredients:

1 kg (2 lbs) spaghetti melon
or pumpkin

2 liters (2 quarts) water

1 tbs salt

1 tsp nutmeg

1 tsp white pepper

1 cup (4 oz) grated
mozzarella cheese

2 tbs tomato purée

3 tbs matza meal or bread
crumbs

Directions:

Spaghetti squash is like a small oval pumpkin with a bright orange fibrous pulp.

Cut horizontally in halves and boil in salted water for 20 minutes. (If using pumpkin instead of squash, boil pumpkin and grate coarsely). Remove seeds with a spoon and twist a fork in to remove pulp from skin (it looks like golden spaghetti and is rich in vitamin A).

Mix with salt and pepper, nutmeg, cheese and tomato purée. Set in an oven-proof dish.

Sprinkle with matza meal or bread crumbs. Bake in oven at 175°C (350°F) for 20 minutes.

Can also be used as a filling in omelettes or vegetable quiches.

Potato Chops
Vegetable-filled Croquettes
Makes 12

PARVE

Ingredients:

1 kg (2 lbs) potatoes
1 cup olive oil
500 g (1 lb) mushrooms
1 clove of garlic, crushed
1 large onion
1 tsp coriander
½ tsp ground ginger
Salt and pepper
200 g (8 oz) green peas and
  diced carrots
2 eggs
Approx. 1 cup matza meal or
  bread crumbs.

MEAT

*The filling mentioned on
page 70 can be used
instead, if a meat dish is
desired.*

*This dish can also be
prepared as explained in
Shepherd's Pie on page 70.*

*Potato chops is a delicious
first course or luncheon
meal.*

Directions:

Wash the potatoes and boil them with a little salt until cooked.

Meanwhile, prepare the filling:

Wash the mushrooms under cold water and dice them very finely.

Peel and chop onion.

Heat ½ cup olive oil in a pot. Sauté the onion and mushrooms, stirring well.

Add the spices, peas and carrots.

Allow to simmer for 10 minutes.

Remove pot from the heat and place on a slant.

Gather the filling to the upper half of the slant so the oil will flow downwards, while the filling cools.

Peel the potatoes and mash with a fork.

Mix 1 egg and 2 tbs matza meal into the mashed potatoes. Season with salt and pepper.

Mix well into a dough.

Divide the dough into balls the size of a ping pong ball.

Wet hands with oil and flatten each ball on the palm of your hand.

Put 1 tbs of the filling in the middle and close around with the potato carefully. Flatten a bit like a thick burger, without damaging the potato covering.

Coat each croquette with beaten egg and then with bread crumbs.

Heat the remaining oil in a frying pan and fry carefully on both sides until brown, approx. 3 min. on each side.

PARVE

Tomato Mousse

Serves 6-8

Ingredients:

2 tsp vegetable soup mix

1 cup water

1 onion, grated

2 envelopes gelatin (28 g
   or 1 oz) (see page 12)

2 cups canned crushed
   tomatoes

Salt and pepper

Juice of 1 lemon

¼ cup mayonnaise

Optional

½ tsp cayenne pepper

Garnish and filling:

3 ripe avocados

1 tbs mayonnaise

3 hard-boiled eggs

Lemon

Salt and pepper

Dill

DAIRY

*If tomato mousse is served
with a dairy dinner,
substitute the mayonnaise
with sour cream.*

Directions:

Boil vegetable soup powder and onion in water.

Sprinkle gelatin powder and stir ingredients frequently.

Add the crushed tomatoes, lemon juice, salt to taste, pepper and cayenne pepper.

Allow to simmer for 3-4 minutes, while stirring frequently.

Remove from the heat and allow to cool until lukewarm.

Beat in mayonnaise.

Rinse a gelatin mold with cold water and pour the tomato mixture in.

Cover with foil and allow to chill for at least 4-5 hours until gelled.

Mash avocados with mayonnaise, eggs, lemon juice, salt and pepper.

To unmold, dip the mold in warm water and loosen sides with a sharp knife.

Invert onto a serving plate.

Put the filling inside, if the mold is a ring shape, or around the mousse, if not.

"By the rivers of Babylon, there we sat down, and we wept, when we remembered Zion."

Psalms, Chapter 137, Verse 1

Tishah B'Av

During the month of *Av* (July/August), the Jews mourn the **destruction of the First and Second Temples** in Jerusalem on the 9th of the month.

Since then, the day has been one of fasting and is called in Hebrew, *Tishah B'Av.*

In the year 586 B.C.E, 400 years after King Solomon constructed his magnificent Temple, the Babylonian king Nebucadnezzer destroyed it for the first time despite the brave defense by the citizens of Jerusalem. At the same time, many were taken prisoner and transferred to Babylon where they yearned... for Jerusalem.

When only forty years later, King Cyrus of Persia conquered Babylon, the Jews were allowed to return to Israel, where they started to build the second Temple. It was inaugurated in the year 516 B.C.E.

The centuries to come were dramatic:

First the Greeks and then the Romans expanded their Empires to include the Jewish realm. The Roman Emperor Vespasian became increasingly aggressive, conquering all of Israel except for Jerusalem. He attacked the city in the year 70 C.E. On the 9th of Av, despite heroic resistance from the Jews, the Roman legions breached their defenses and wreaked destruction on the city and the Temple. Only the outer western wall was saved from destruction. It is this original part, commonly known as the Wailing Wall, or the **Kotel**, which still exists in Jerusalem and is one of the most moving and significant Jewish holy sites.

Exciting archaeological excavations have confirmed recently that a dynamic cultural and religious life took place around the Temple. On the **9th of Av,** the prophet Jeremiah's Book of Lamentations *(Eicha)* and the verses of Elegy *(Kinot)* are read in all synagogues to remind us of the destruction of the First and Second Temples.

There is a tradition that **no meat dishes** are eaten during the first nine days of the months of Av, except on Shabbat.

"... wheat, barley, meal, parched grain, beans and lentils ..."
Samuel II, Chapter 17, Verse 28
From Shobi's "shopping list" for King David's desert refuge

These days are a period of mourning, and we abstain from extra pleasures and festivities.

In India, we children were served a special dish to symbolize humility, since it is eaten by millions of poor Indians every day – if they have anything to eat at all!

We liked this dish very much, and didn't feel humble or poor at all when we ate it. We lived in an apartment building with many large families of 8 or 9 children.

Since there was not much room in the small apartments, we children often met in "our hallway".

Each child had his or her plate of food. We sat crosslegged on the floor and ate with our fingers.

I should add that there was a special set of manners for "eating with your fingers". We only used our right hands and only the finger tips. Neatly and daintily, we gathered a small ball of rice and sauce in a piece of *chapati* (Indian bread) and put it gracefully into our mouths!

We always had a glass of cold water beside us.

The dish is called *Dahl Chaval* (ch as in Charlie). (See following page 169.)

Dahl Chaval

Red Lentils and Rice

Serves 4

PARVE

Ingredients:

1³/₄ cups red lentils
2-3 cm (1½") piece of fresh
  ginger or 1 tsp ground
  ginger
2 cups water
1 tsp salt
1-2 tbs oil
1 small onion
1 clove of garlic
¼ tsp red pepper or chili
  powder
½ tsp oriental cumin
1-2 tbs tomato paste
1 tbs seasoned vinegar

PARVE

Variation:
For a more filling meal,
serve half a hard-boiled
egg per person or chickpea
"meatballs" (Falafel – page
174).

Directions:

Pick over the lentils and remove any pebbles, straw, etc.

Rinse 2-3 times in cold water.

Cook the lentils with ginger and salt for approx. 10 minutes, only partially covered, to prevent the lentils from boiling over. Skim the surface.

While the lentils are cooking, prepare the *massala* (dressing).

Heat the oil in a pot. Slice the onion in rings and fry with the garlic, stirring well.

Add all the spices and the cooked lentils, mixing well to give the consistency of oatmeal.

Serve with hot rice, cooked in plenty of salted water.

Allow ½ cup raw rice per person.

Cook for about 15 minutes and drain.

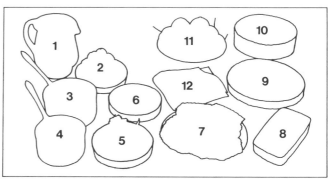

Av

PARVE

Suki Baji
Spicy Potato Salad
Makes 6-8

Ingredients:

1 kg (2 lb) small firm
  potatoes
1 tsp coriander powder
½ tsp cumin
1 tsp ground white pepper
1 tsp salt
2 tbs oil
½ tsp turmeric
2 tbs chopped fresh
  coriander or dill
Juice of ½ lemon

Optional:

½ tsp cayenne pepper
½ tsp white mustard seeds

Directions:

Boil potatoes until cooked. Peel and dice.

Season with coriander powder, cumin, white pepper, salt and cayenne pepper (if desired).

Heat oil in a pot. Add turmeric. Stir well and sprinke with mustard seeds. Reduce heat.

Put in the seasoned potatoes and turn them around carefully in the pot – until they get warm.

When serving, sprinkle with chopped fresh coriander and lemon juice.

Can be eaten either warm or cold, with chapati (Indian bread - see below).

Chapati
Indian Bread
Makes 12

PARVE

Ingredients:

1 cup graham (wholewheat)
  flour
3 cups white flour
1 tbs oil
1½ cups water
2 tbs parve margarine
1 tsp salt

Directions:

Combine graham and white flour with salt in a bowl.

Make a well in the middle.

Pour water and oil in and knead into a soft dough.

Cover with a damp cloth and allow to rise for 30 min.

Divide the dough into 12 balls.

Roll out flat circles of about 2 mm (⅛") thick.

Heat a heavy-bottomed pan and melt a little margarine in it. Fry the chapaties one at a time, approx. 1 minute on each side.

Then, hold chapati with tongs over a gas flame until it puffs up, or place under a hot grill for a few seconds.

When ready, place on a large plate and cover.

Chapati tastes best when very fresh.

Kitchree

Red Lentils and Rice

Serves 8

Ingredients:

2 tbs parve margarine
2 cloves of garlic, crushed
½ tsp cumin
½ tsp pepper
1 tsp salt
3 tomatoes
1 tbs tomato purée
2 cups rice
½ cup red lentils
3 cups water

Red lentils (Kitchree) have a strong smell and taste. We usually ate Kitchree around the 9th of Av (commemorating the destruction of the 1st and 2nd Temples) as it is traditional to eat non-meat meals.

Variation:
Kitchree tastes good with a fried egg or falafel (see next page) and chutney.

Directions:

Clean the red lentils and remove stones.

Melt margarine in a pot.

Add garlic, cumin, pepper and salt.

Dice tomatoes.

Mix with tomato purée and stir in spices.

Wash rice and lentils in cold water, drain in colander and add to the sauce in the pot.

Pour in water and stir all ingredients well.

Cover and bring to boil and then simmer for 20 minutes.

Stir before serving.

My Mother's Falafel
Chick pea Balls
Makes 30

Ingredients:
1¾ cups dry chickpeas
2 large onions
2 tbs parsley or dill, chopped
1 tsp pepper
½ tsp chili
1 tsp ground ginger
1 tsp coriander
½ tsp cumin
1 tsp salt
3 tbs flour
½ tsp bicarbonate of soda

For frying:
¾ cup vegetable oil

Directions:

Soak the chickpeas overnight in water and a little salt.

Drain and grind the chickpeas, together with the peeled onions.

Add all the remaining ingredients.

Mix well and allow to chill 10 minutes before forming (with moist fingers) small balls.

Deep-fry the falafel in hot oil until golden brown in color.

Remove to absorbent paper.

Serve warm with pita, salad and tehina dressing (see next page).

If more convenient, form small flat cakes and fry in hot oil or margarine in a frying pan.

Thanks to good travel opportunities and many young travelers, knowledge of Israeli foods has grown. Israeli falafel has become well known in many other countries.
Portions of falafel consist of: (a) Pitot (plural of "pita", the round bread with a pocket) filled with
(b) falafel, which are fried chickpea balls,
(c) fresh salad – usually cucumber, tomatoes, onion, green peppers – all very finely diced,
(d) different dressings – mostly tehina (sesame seed paste – diluted with lemon juice) and spices, and
(e) zchug – a chilli purée seasoned with salt, lemon juice and spices (for the more daring palate!).

One can, of course, bake the pitot at home. However, since it is popular and easily obtainable in most markets, I suggest buying them ready made and always having some in the freezer. They can be warmed up in a toaster for 3-4 minutes and then taste freshly baked. Some are made with white flour and others with whole wheat.

Tehina Dressing for Falafel

Serves 4

PARVE

Ingredients:
½ cup tehina paste
½ cup water
1 clove of garlic, crushed
1 pinch of cayenne pepper
1 tsp salt
Juice of 1-2 lemons
1-2 tbs chopped parsley

Directions:
Put all ingredients except the parsley into the blender and blend to a fine paste.

When serving, add the chopped parsley into the sauce or as a garnish.

PARVE

Tehina Paste:
This is one part sesame seeds and one part water, blended to a fine paste. Concentrated tehina can be found in most health shops and needs to be diluted with water and lemon juice before use.

Salad for Falafel

Directions:
Finely dice: tomatoes, fresh peppers, cucumber, onion, etc.

Mix together and dress with oil, lemon, salt and pepper, if eaten separately. Otherwise, place into the pita pocket with the falafel balls and dress with tehina.

DAIRY

Chilled Fish Mousse
Serves 10-12

Ingredients:
1 kg (2 lbs) fillets of fish
  (cod, plaice or herring)
2 carrots
1 large onion
4 bay leaves
6 peppercorns
3 tbs lemon juice
3 envelopes kosher gelatin –
  14 g (½ oz) each
½ cup dry white wine
1 tsp salt
2 tbs chives, chopped
2 tbs dill, chopped
1 tbs mustard powder
1 tbs ground white pepper
1 cup whipping cream

Garnish:
Lemon slices
Dill
Lettuce leaves

> **When serving:**
> **Release fish mousse from mold by dipping the mold into a bowl of hot water. Loosen sides with a sharp knife and invert onto serving dish and garnish.**

Directions:
Put the fish, carrots, onion, bay leaves, peppercorns and lemon juice in a pot. Add 2 cups water and bring slowly to boil. Allow to simmer for 30 minutes.

Dissolve 1 package gelatin powder in ¼ cup water. Allow to soften for 10 minutes. In another pot, heat ½ cup fish stock (from above) and ½ cup wine and then add gelatin mixture. Heat until gelatin is completely dissolved.

Allow to cool to a syrupy consistency.

Slice one of the boiled carrots and arrange in desired pattern on the bottom of a mold (round or rectangle).

Pour the gelatin over the carrots and allow to gel in the fridge.

Meanwhile, take the fish out of the stock. Remove small bones completely! Grind fish in a chopper or grinder together with the carrots and onions.

Season with salt, pepper, chives, dill and mustard powder.

Now, warm 1 cup of fish stock with the 2 remaining envelopes of gelatin powder until the gelatin dissolves.

Then, pour into the fish purée while stirring very well.

Whip cream to soft peaks, and fold into the fish.

Pour the fish mousse over the chilled jelly in the mold and allow to chill again for 3-4 hours.

Unmold and garnish.

Apples in Syrup
For Rosh Hashanah
Approx. 1 kg (2 lbs)

PARVE

Ingredients:

1 kg (2 lbs) firm apples
  (Golden Delicious)
2-3 quinces (to give color)
3 tsp "calcium powder" (can
  be bought at a pharmacy)
1½ liter (1½ quart) water
400 g (1 lb) sugar
½ tsp citric acid
½ tsp cardamom

---

*The Hebrew month of Elul,
which falls during the
month of August or
September, is the last
month before the Jewish
New Year. Preparations for
the coming year are about
to start and the beautiful
notes of the ram's horn are
heard in the synagogue,
reminding us that the Holy
Days of the New Year and
the Days of Awe are close at
hand.
In my childhood home in
India, these days of Elul
were filled with the
delicious aroma of apples
being cooked in a special
syrup, in preparation for
the New Year's Celebration.*

Directions:

Stir the calcium powder in 1½ liter of water in a large bowl. The powder prevents the apples from getting too soft.

Peel, core and cut the apples in wedges. Poke with a fork in 3-4 places on each wedge. Quarter the quinces.

Soak the fruit in the calcium water and stir with every new addition.

Keep the fruit in the water for ½ an hour.

Mix the sugar with 2 cups water in a pot and bring to a boil until the sugar dissolves.

Wash the fruit a few times in fresh water, then add it to the syrup.

Partly cover the pot and bring to boiling point.

Allow to boil for 10 minutes.

Stir the pot carefully and reduce heat.

Allow fruit to simmer for 15 minutes.

Mix the citric acid in ½ cup water and pour into the syrup. Allow to simmer on low heat for about an hour.

Add cardamom and shake the pot (stirring at this point might damage the fruit).

Turn off the heat after 10 minutes when the apple syrup gets a golden color.

Keep in a clean jar, tightly closed.

177

The History of the Bagel

Bagel is a Yiddish word and there are many different explanations for its origin. Some interpretations even include mystic symbols. Some people believe the word originates from the German word "beugel" meaning a ring or bracelet. Others believe the word is derived from an old Austrian word "buegel" which means stirrup.

In Krakow, as early as 1610, bagels were mentioned in literature as a symbol of the continuation of life and the boundlessness of the universe. The round form was supposed to bring future happiness. Bread formed in a circle was eaten following both childbirth and funerals. This has been linked to a reference in King Solomon's Ecclesiastes: *"Generations go, generations come, but the Universe remains forever."*

Today, the word bagel refers to a ring of soft bread, baked with a golden brown crust. The Eastern European Jews brought their favorite bagel recipes to the United States at the beginning of this century, and a wide variety of bagels can be found at breakfast counters and delicatessens throughout the U.S.

Traditionally, bagels are made with gluten-enriched white flour. However, for health reasons, different ingredients may be substituted, including whole wheat and other types of flours. Toasted bagels with cream cheese and lox (smoked salmon) are a traditional Sunday brunch delicacy, not only in Jewish homes, but in many fine restaurants and hotels.

ELUL

Bagels

Makes 20

PARVE

Ingredients:

25 g (1 oz) yeast
2 tsp sugar
1½ cups water
3 tbs oil
1 tsp salt
1 egg
4 cups flour

For cooking:

3 liters (3 quarts) water
1 tbs salt

Garnish:

Coarse salt
Caraway or poppy seeds.

Directions:

Dissolve yeast in ½ cup lukewarm water and 1 teaspoon sugar.

Allow to stand 5 minutes. Combine flour, salt, and 1 teaspoon sugar in a large bowl and make a well in the middle.

Pour in 1 cup lukewarm water together with yeast and water mixture.

Add oil and egg.

Knead all ingredients to a soft dough.

Cover with a clean damp cloth.

Allow to rise for 45 minutes.

Knead the dough on a floured board and form small sausages of approx. 13 cm (5") long and 2 cm (1") thick. Bring edges together to form a ring and press firmly.

Put on a baking tray lined with baking paper, cover and leave for 10 minutes.

Bring 3 liters (3 quarts) of water and 1 tablespoon salt to a boil.

Drop the rings in carefully and allow to cook for 2-3 minutes.

Lift them up with the help of a perforated ladle and place again on baking sheet.

Sprinkle with salt or poppy seeds and bake in preheated oven at 200°C (400°F) for 20-25 minutes.

179

PARVE

Walnut Bread

2-4 breads

Ingredients:
Sourdough:
2 cups rye flour

*1 cup water (mixed in a
bowl and allowed to
leaven for at least 48
hours)*

Then add the following:
*1 bottle black beer (sweet
and nonalcoholic)*

1¼ cup lukewarm water

25 g (1 oz) yeast

1 tbs salt

About 1 kg (2 lbs) flour

1 cup chopped walnuts

---

*When I bake rye bread (see
next page), I usually take 2
portions (1½ cup each) of
sourdough from the dough
before forming into breads.
One portion I use for rye-
bread and the other in
walnut bread or sometimes
substitute the walnuts with
sunflower seeds. A slice of
walnut bread with cold
butter makes a delicious
treat with tea or coffee.*

Directions:
Mix sourdough, beer, water, yeast and salt in a large bowl.

Add flour and nuts gradually, and knead until the dough slips from the bowl. If still sticky, add more flour.

Form a big ball. Cover with a damp cloth and keep at room temperature for 1½ hours.

Knead on a floured board. You might need more flour.

Divide into 2 or 4 portions as desired. Form into round or long breads.

Place breads on a baking tray lined with baking paper. Cut 3-4 shallow slits on each bread and allow to rise again (covered with a damp cloth) for 30 minutes.

Brush breads with water before putting in a preheated oven. Bake at 200°C (400°F) for 50 minutes, if divided into 4 breads, or an hour if divided into 2.

Rye Bread with Sourdough

3 Breads

PARVE

Ingredients:
Sourdough
2 cups rye flour
1 cup water

**Then the following
ingredients are added:**
2 liters (2 quarts) water
5 g (¹/₅ oz) yeast (only the first
  time)
1 kg (2 lb) crushed rye grains
4 cups white flour
3 tbs coarse salt
1 kg (2 lb) rye flour
1 bottle black beer or 1½ cups
  water
Approx. 1 cup mixed seeds
  (sunflower, flax, sesame)

Optional:
Hazelnuts

---

*Baking rye bread is not
difficult, and it gets better the
more you bake.
Remove a small amount of
dough (1½ cups) every time
and keep stored in the
refrigerator for the next time.
All you need is a large bowl
that can contain 6-8 liters (6-8
quarts) and 3 good bread tins
with non-stick lining.
Otherwise remember to grease
ordinary tins very well and
sprinkle flour to avoid bread
sticking to sides and bottom!
Regular baking keeps the
sourdough going and the
results get better every time.*

Directions:
Mix rye flour and water in a bowl and allow to leaven for at least 48 hours, covered and at room temperature.

Then mix sourdough with water, yeast, crushed rye grains, white flour and salt and put in a large bowl. (Yeast is used only the first time – later sourdough taken from the dough will be enough to start a new dough.)

Cover the bowl with a damp cloth and allow to leaven again for 12-24 hours (depending how sour one likes the bread).

Then add black beer or water, rye flour, water and seeds.

Now, take 1½ cups of the dough and put it in a jar or glass with a lid. Sprinkle with coarse salt to help it keep better and store in refrigerator until needed. It will keep for 14 days in the refrigerator.

If hazelnuts are desired in the bread , they can be added to the dough at this stage. The dough should be divided into 3 well-greased bread tins.

Cover breads again with damp cloth and allow to rise for 2-6 hours.

Poke with a fork or skewer. Bake on the lowest shelf of a preheated oven at 100°C (200°F) for 1 hour and then raise the heat to 200°C (400°F) for a further 1½ hours.

Remove the baked bread from the forms and pack in the damp cloth that has been rinsed in cold water.

Allow breads to cool completely packed in damp cloths.

Breads

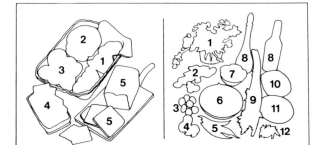

Spices

1. Fresh Coriander
2. Fresh Ginger Root
3. Pecan Nuts
4. Garlic
5. Green Chilis
6. On the Plate: Bay Leaves, Coriander
   Seeds, Saffron, Cinnamon,
   Nutmeg, Cardamom and Cloves

7. Fennel Seeds
8. Vinegar
9. Fresh Celery
10. Coconut
11. Red Chilis
12. Curry Leaves

My Spice Rack

There are many exotic spices on the market, and their aromatic smell attracts one, especially the fresh herbs at the green grocer or vegetable section in supermarkets.

Food prepared with fresh herbs and spices has a more appetizing aroma than those seasoned with ground dried spices packed in plastic or glass because spices tend to lose flavor in such containers.

Some spices which are now available fresh are: ginger root, coconut cream, coriander and fresh chillies.

In all my recipes I have suggested smaller amounts of the strong spices to suit those unaccustomed to hot food. But for the more daring, I would suggest adding spices according to taste. In case one goes too far, a squirt of fresh lemon juice can neutralize the taste.

Here are some "uncommon" spices from my spice rack and I hope they will serve as an inspiration:

Aniseed: Small dry seeds, they smell and taste of licorice. Used in vegetable cutlets or dishes.

Cardamom: Small dried pods with seeds inside, has a lovely aroma, available whole, dried or ground. A *must* in most Indian dishes, one ingredient of garam massala - used in sweetmeats and pastry.

Cayenne pepper: From the same family as green and red chilis. Strong taste, should be used sparingly.

Chili: Red hot pepper, like cayenne, should be used sparingly.

Cinnamon: Dried red/brown bark available in sticks or ground, used as part of garam massala, or in ground meat, rice and pastry. Should be used sparingly as it dominates the smell of the food.

Cloves: Resembles small brown "nails", and is available whole or ground, use sparingly as the smell and taste can easily dominate other ingredients. One of ingredients of garam massala. In the Orient, cloves are chewed to freshen breath.

Coconut cream: Relatively new on the market, pressed coconut, easy to use, melts quickly in warm dishes, gives an exotic aroma in fish curry, and in spicy dishes.

Coriander: Available fresh, resembles parsley but has a stronger smell and taste. Can be planted indoors in flower pots. Available also as whole seeds or ground; an important spice in curry dishes.

Cumin: Resembles caraway seeds, but has a special exotic taste and smell, used in most Indian and Middle Eastern dishes usually combined with ground coriander. Used in beans and lentils.

Curry leaves: Strong curry smelling leaves, available fresh and dried in Indian spice shops. Used in meat or fish curry and in legumes and potatoes.

Curry powder: A ready mixture of different Indian spices, available in many variations. By combining one's favorite spices, one can find one's special "massala" (blend).

Fennel: Licorice taste and smell - used in many Oriental pastries.

Garam Massala: A mixture of different spices such as: pepper, nutmeg, cardamom, cinnamon and cloves. Used in meat or poultry dishes and Indian rice pilaf.

Ginger root: Available fresh, dried or ground, it gives a strong fresh taste and aroma to food or drink, and also works as meat tenderizer and as a digestive.

Mint: Available fresh, grows easily in the garden or indoors; used in sweet and sour dishes, tea and as aromatic garnish on salads. Tastes best fresh. Available also dried.

Mustard seeds: White or dark red/brown tiny round seeds, used in pickles and potatoes, very strong in taste.

Nutmeg: Available as whole nuts or ground. Has a sweet spicy aroma. Used mostly in Oriental sweetmeats or chutney.

Rosewater: Originally made by cooking fresh rose petals. Available at the pharmacy, it gives a smell of rose. Used mostly in Oriental sweetmeats.

Saffron: Orange red filament from the pistil of the crocus flower. Expensive spice, used sparingly to give the food a golden red color and mild flavor. Available in different qualities.

Tamarind: Brown tropical fruit. Available dried (like dates, figs etc.) or as a concentrated paste. Gives the food a sour taste and brown color, available in shops selling Indian spices.

Turmeric: Hard orange root ground to powder, colors the food yellow. Should be sautéed in oil before adding other spices.

Wine in Judaism

Noah was the first wine maker! Since then, wine is mentioned many times in the Bible:

When two of the twelve scouts returned to the Israelites in the desert, they brought back huge bunches of grapes as an example of the fruitfulness of the land the Israelites were about to enter.

The grape is one of the seven fruits for which Israel was famous throughout history, and grape wine has always had a special meaning in Judaism. It is used for blessings on Shabbat and other holidays, and all festive occasions.

During the Pesach Seder, one should drink four glasses of wine or grape juice. For Purim, it is permitted to drink beyond thirst to celebrate the happy occasion when the Jews of Persia were rescued.

L'Chaim - to life - is the traditional Jewish "Cheers!"

At the *Brit Mila*, the circumcision ceremony, the eight-day-old boy gets a drop of wine on his lips.

Under the *Hupa*, or canopy at a wedding ceremony, the bride and groom share their first glass of wine, as a symbol of a fruitful future together.

After a Jewish wedding, the newlyweds are traditionally honored by seven days of feasting, *Sheva Brachot* (Seven Blessings), where the joyful occasion is celebrated with food, wine and wishes of health and happiness.

For wine to be kosher, it is controlled from harvesting to serving at the table. Today, a large variety of kosher wines is available with the selection increasing constantly, mainly from Israel, whose wines are exported to all over the world.

The law of Kashrut applies to all wine containing grapes, while alcoholic beverages of other fruits are not included.

In India, kosher wine was not available, so we made our own raisin juice to be used for Shabbat prayers. Perhaps this simple recipe will tempt others who prefer a non-alcoholic drink:

Bombay Raisin Juice

Directions:
Wash the raisins thoroughly and soak in water until the following day.

Crush the raisins and strain.

The juice is sweet and should be kept cool.

Ingredients:
1 dl (½ cup) dark raisins
2 dl (1 cup) water

The leftover raisins and juice were gathered and stored in a clay pot for months until they became sour, producing a fine vinegar.

186

Weights & Measurements

All spoon & cup measurements are level.

The Quarts & Pints in this book are U.S. measurements.

100 ml	= 1 dl
10 dl	= 1 liter
1 pint (U.S.)	= 0.47 liter (appr. ½ liter)
1 pint (Engl.)	= 0.57 liter
1 Quart (U.S.)	= 0.95 liter
1 Quart (Engl.)	= 1.15 liter
1 lb	= 454 gram (g)
1 oz	= 28 gram (g)
1 cup	= 2½ dl = 250 ml
1 tbs	= 20 ml
1 tsp	= 5 ml

Temperatures / Oven

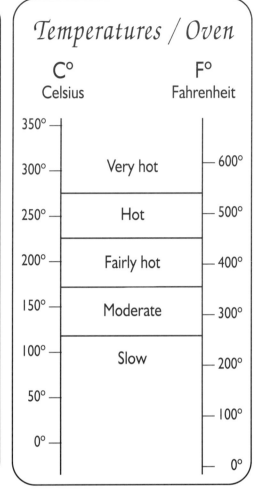

C° Celsius		F° Fahrenheit
350°		
300°	Very hot	600°
250°	Hot	500°
200°	Fairly hot	400°
150°	Moderate	300°
100°	Slow	200°
50°		100°
0°		0°

Abbreviations

l	= liter	tbs	= tablespoon
dl	= deciliter	tsp	= teaspoon
ml	= milliliter	C°	= Celsius
kg	= kilogram	F°	= Fahrenheit
g	= gram		
oz	= ounce		

Index

189

Color Photo Chart

What the Danish critics say:

Berlingske Tidende
(leading conservative paper)

"This a good book and you don't have to be Jewish to enjoy it. Most people buy cookbooks about Greek, Italian, Indian, Chinese, Japanese and French cooking without thinking twice. This is why a truly delightful and inspiring Jewish cookbook also ought to take its natural place on the bookshelf. And the food is even simple to prepare!"

Politiken
(leading liberal paper)

"Mention Jewish food and most Danes will immediately think of bagels, chopped liver, and other Eastern European foods. There isn't only one Jewish cuisine, but many cuisines whose recipes reflect the countries where they were created and the available ingredients. The book certainly will attract non-Jewish cooks as well, to try out Jewish cuisine à la "Bachmann".

Hotel & Restaurant
(leading trade magazine)

"My Jewish Cuisine - For All Seasons" is an exciting and highly international Jewish cookbook. In addition to exotic dishes, the book includes a section on Jewish dietary laws, the Jewish calendar, and the respective holidays."

Frederiksborg Amtavis
(newspaper for the fashionable nothern Copenhagen suburbs)

"The author introduces the reader to international kosher gastronomy, and anyone who likes exciting dishes can use her cookbook. Of course, there is nothing to keep a non-Jew from enjoying Jewish food. The recipes are arranged as entire meals for the Sabbath and holidays, with instructions on how to proceed with each."

Hjemkundskab
(magazine for economics teachers)

"My Jewish Cuisine is a cookbook far above the ordinary. While readers are given recipes for a large number of exciting and exotic foods, they are also introduced to the history of Jewish culture and religion. The book's numerous original recipes carefully adhere to traditional Jewish dietary rules, but in a manner that makes for exciting eating for nutrition-conscious people. I can give this book my warmest recommendation for usage at schools and professional libraries. A reader who is interested in food and different cultures can look forward to a truly memorable personal experience."